To Theresa
You are Love.

Love never dies.

Love,
Mary ♡ ♡ ♡

Hospice memories . com

Messages FROM THE Afterlife

MEMOIRS OF A HOSPICE NURSE

Mary Hill

BALBOA.
PRESS
A DIVISION OF HAY HOUSE

Balboa Press books may be ordered through booksellers or by contacting:

Balboa Press
A Division of Hay House
1663 Liberty Drive
Bloomington, IN 47403
www.balboapress.com
1 (877) 407-4847

Because of the dynamic nature of the Internet, any web addresses or links contained in this book may have changed since publication and may no longer be valid. The views expressed in this work are solely those of the author and do not necessarily reflect the views of the publisher, and the publisher hereby disclaims any responsibility for them.

The author of this book does not dispense medical advice or prescribe the use of any technique as a form of treatment for physical, emotional, or medical problems without the advice of a physician, either directly or indirectly. The intent of the author is only to offer information of a general nature to help you in your quest for emotional and spiritual well-being. In the event you use any of the information in this book for yourself, which is your constitutional right, the author and the publisher assume no responsibility for your actions.

Print information available on the last page.

ISBN: 978-1-9822-0201-9 (sc)
ISBN: 978-1-9822-0200-2 (hc)
ISBN: 978-1-9822-0202-6 (e)

Library of Congress Control Number: 2018904103

Balboa Press rev. date: 04/10/2018

Contents

ENDORSEMENTS VII

DEDICATION. IX

ACKNOWLEDGEMENTS. XI

INTRODUCTION XIII

PART 1
Hospice Patient Stories

Chapter 1   How It All Began 1

Chapter 2   Jeff. 4

Chapter 3   Dennis 7

Chapter 4   Lil. 10

Chapter 5   Walt 16

Chapter 6   Pamela 18

Chapter 7   Lillie 21

Chapter 8   Emily 23

Chapter 9   Rosemary. 26

Chapter 10   Carolyn 29

Chapter 11   Ngoc. 31

Chapter 12   Loretta. 35

Chapter 13   Billie. 38

Part 2
My Journey

Chapter 14   Strawberry Music Festival 42

Chapter 15   Facing Fears. 44

Chapter 16   Family 46

Chapter 17   My Shamanic Path 49

Chapter 18   Taking Care of Myself 55

Chapter 19   Fears. 58

Chapter 20   Past Lives... 62

Chapter 21   Hospice Per Diem 64

Chapter 22   Mom's Decline...................................... 67

Chapter 23   My Nursing History................................ 69

Chapter 24   The Joys of Per Diem Hospice....................... 72

Chapter 25   Letting Go and Letting God 73

Chapter 26   Dorothy 76

Chapter 27   My Chicago Visit.................................... 79

Chapter 28   Quitting Hospice.................................... 83

Chapter 29   Dorothy's Transition 85

Chapter 30   Christmas Eve....................................... 88

Chapter 31   Fears Around Money 89

Chapter 32   Dorothy's Return.................................... 91

Chapter 33   Chicago Trip for Mother's Day 93

Chapter 34   Mom on Hospice 96

Chapter 35   A Letter to Mikey 104

Chapter 36   Reflections on Life.................................. 106

Chapter 37   Healing Work 109

Chapter 38   Family Dynamics 110

Chapter 39   Retirement 112

Chapter 40   Plant Medicine......................................114

Chapter 41   Alternative Medicine............................... 118

Chapter 42   Blessings of Being a Hospice Nurse................... 120

Chapter 43   Benefits of Cannabis 123

Chapter 44   Love 125

Chapter 45   Pain Medications................................... 129

Chapter 46   Gratitude 133

Chapter 47   More Reflections on Life 136

Chapter 48   Lessons I Learned from Hospice 142

Chapter 49   Self Love 145

Chapter 50   Mom's Decline..................................... 147

Chapter 51   Home Again.. 152

Chapter 52   Losing My Mom 158

Chapter 53   Aftermath.. 171

EPILOGUE 187

Endorsements

"Mary's beautiful book helps us to remember that death is but a change and not an end. Real communication happens soul-to-soul – whether we are in a body or not."

With love,
Robert Holden
Author of *Shift Happens!* and *Life Loves You,* co-written with Louise Hay

"I admire the depth of courage and presence it takes to be there for people who are dying and to counsel their families during this very challenging process. Mary Hill shares her experiences and magical moments that allow death and dying to be embraced through the lens of love. It gifts the reader with a release from fear as she lets us know, without a doubt, that life lives on beyond our physical bodies. She opens the door for us to see great beauty and grace for all involved if we choose to allow it."

Shawn Gallaway
Award-winning singer/songwriter and author of *I Choose Love*
www.ShawnGallaway.com

"Mary is a pure channel of divine love and light. In this book, you gain a glimpse into the life of a true healer – her simplicity and purity – as well as discover what's on the other side of death. See what a modern-day saint who lives the truth of love looks like. Mary is a remarkable woman who reminds me of Mother Theresa or Mother Mary. She is a mother of all beings – a woman who has kissed the foreheads of the dying and mourned each passing as if it was that of her own child. Her humility and love shine through."

Love, Love, Love & More Love,
Dr. Wendy Treynor
Author of *The Gift of Cancer: Turn your Tragedy into a Treasure ... A Treasure Map to Happiness*
www.ICanHeal.com

"This is a story about the power of compassion and understanding. Mary Hill takes the reader through the emotional complexities of nursing in a hospice. She deals with life and death with skill, insight and empathy. A powerful read that you cannot put down."

John M. Haggerty
Author and Entrepreneur
Angels Camp, Ca

"My mother passed away, unexpectedly, within 10 days – the same year as Mary's mother. On the final day and feeling spiritually bankrupt, I just needed some reassuring, comfort and guidance. Being miles apart, our phone call grounded me for the day's events that were angelic in nature.

Mary's gift and passion for Life radiates within the fullness of her heart. One will feel the love through the pages of her magical journey. Again, and again, Mary "shows up with love" – one of her favorite mantras that she shares consistently with others. Mary IS Love!"

Sunshine Always ~
Sharyn L Hampton
Educator, Entrepreneur, Health Coach
www.SharynLHampton.com

Dedication

To all my hospice families and patients who taught me what love looks like.

Acknowledgements

I would like to thank Lainey Johns who was a huge help in the development of my book. She helped me during the early author submission process that I was too scared to figure out on my own. She transcribed my voice recordings and handwritten journal entries that were contained in various loose-leaf papers and spiral notebooks. Her beautiful butterfly artwork became the cover for the book and she helped with the early editing process.

I am grateful for my wonderful husband, Gary, for his love, support and editing through this entire long process. He has lived this hospice journey with me and has been my rock through the trials and tribulations of my career and life.

Many thanks to my awesome friends and family for their valuable feedback, encouragement and support when I did not think I could go on.

I am so grateful to my friend Sharyn Hampton for the many hours she spent with the final editing of my book. Her love and friendship are gifts that I treasure.

I am very appreciative of the wonderful people at Balboa Press who assisted me with editing my manuscript and publishing this book.

Introduction

I have been spiritual since my teenage years and was fascinated with the concept of death and dying. I read many books on the subject, but still had fear about my own death.

I began my hospice career in 1997 as a Case Manager caring for terminally ill patients. I began journaling my experiences with one of my earliest patients, Jeff. I placed that story into a manila folder entitled "My Book" and filed it away. I thought that maybe someday I would write a book about hospice nursing. I was not called to resume writing again until 10 years later.

The first four years of being a Case Manager was spent seeing patients in their homes. I loved my job, but I began feeling drained from all the deaths I had witnessed. I needed a change.

For the next five years, I had various jobs with the same company as an Admissions Nurse, a Sales and Marketing Associate and a Nurse Liaison. I understood that I was missing the connection with patients and their families, so I decided to return to a Case Manager position for the last four years of my career. That was when the magic started!

I had a life-changing spiritual awakening just days after the 9/11 tragedy. I began to see the world and my own life through new eyes … through the eyes of Love and Oneness and that made all the difference. Once again, I found myself enjoying those close patient and family connections and began journaling my experiences with my patients in earnest.

Part One of my book is about my patient stories that speak of the divine grace that accompanied the dying process. Several of my patients appeared to me, while I was fully awake, in various ways after they passed. This was evidence to me that life, or consciousness, continued after we dropped our physical body. It is my personal belief that love and joy awaits us on the other side.

Part Two of my book is about my journey with my mother's illness and her death. I received messages from my dear mother, Georgia, after she made her transition into the afterlife in 2013. She was on hospice with the Chicago branch of the company I had worked for. It also contains other hospice stories as I continued my career as a per diem nurse; my experience with Reiki and shamanic healing work; facing many of my own fears; and my views on the controversial subject of medical cannabis in treating pain and anxiety as well as my personal experience with cannabis. Further discussion continues with my thoughts about Alternative Medicine versus Western Medicine.

I have had to face my own fears about death and dying, as most people do at some point, but I have come to believe that the concept of death is an illusion. My vision for this book is to help others overcome their natural fears and to shed light on end-of-life issues.

May your hearts be filled with divine grace as you read these stories and possibly address the notion of your own mortality or someone you love.

PART 1

Hospice Patient Stories

CHAPTER 1

How It All Began

My 13 years of working in hospice taught me one thing; there is no death. There is only life – the life we are aware of now and the life beyond our vision. Kathryn Dowling Singh states in her book, *The Grace in Dying*, "The life beyond the veil is a universal process marked primarily by the dissolution of the body, the separate sense of self, and the ascendancy of spirit."

My spiritual awareness began to blossom when I was 14-years-old. I had a vivid dream that my maternal grandmother had died. She lived in San Francisco where my mother grew up. As I made my way to the kitchen in the morning, I found my mother sitting at the kitchen table, sobbing into her folded arms. I went over to her and wrapped my arms around her. I asked her why she was crying and she said, "My mother died." I was stunned. I told my mom about the dream I had that night. We held each other tight as we both cried. That experience started my fascination and curiosity about death.

When I reflected back on my hospice days, my fondest memories were the connections with families and how appreciative they were for the love and support I provided as their RN Case Manager. I never saw my patients as dying patients. I saw them very much alive even though they were facing a terminal diagnosis. I felt honored to make a difference in a time of their lives when they were at their most vulnerable and full of fear. I had seen so much devotion in family members who stayed at the bedside of their loved one, day and night, not wanting to leave. They put their own lives on hold so they could be there for their loved ones.

Many people felt a palpable fear with the approach of death – both the patient and their family members. The person dying reminded family members of their own mortality which was something most people avoided thinking about. However, so many miracles also occurred during the dying process. A sacred space was created in the midst of this divine passage into love and bliss. With all of my experience as a Reiki Master and a Shaman, I was able to encourage this sacred space to occur when patients were ready – and, sometimes, when they were not.

I learned Reiki – which means universal life energy – and had been practicing it for two years. Reiki is a healing technique based on the principle that the therapist could channel energy into the patient by means of touch in order to activate the natural healing process of the patient's body and restore physical and emotional well-being. The Reiki master gives a person an attunement that activates the Reiki energy and spiritual guides are received during this process. It is safe because it simply moves blocked energy that is stored within the body.

I began giving my patients Reiki treatments – with their permission, of course – and saw remarkable results. It normally had a deep, calming effect on a patient who was experiencing anxiety, as many do, especially in their final days. Because I was a channel for God's energy, that energy flowed through me. I felt the tingling in my hands as the energy ran through them.

I realized we were put on this earth to help one another. We were all "one" and the love we shared was what mattered most. I felt greater love for my husband and other family members. I felt more alive and awake. I understood it was not about what my husband was doing or not doing – it was about me. Focusing on him distracted me from my own goals and dreams.

My decision to become a Reiki Master allowed me to set my husband free to live his own life and it set me free to live mine. I could finally be in full recognition of my gifts and talents while pursuing my dreams. I had never been able to articulate what I wanted in life.

I was codependent, being the eldest of five children, and acted like a second mom to my last three siblings when I was just 10-years-old.

My hospice journey started in October 1997 after working in the home health field as a Nurse Case Manager for several terminal patients. I had concerns about whether I could look death in the face every working day and face the pain that I saw in the eyes of loved ones. Nevertheless, I felt drawn to this work and marveled at the miracles that surrounded the dying process. However, I struggled for two years about the decision to join the full-time ranks of the hospice team that was a division of the home health company for which I worked.

The decision became easy when our home health company was being purchased. The hospice division remained a separate business and there was an opening for a hospice nurse. I applied for the position and was hired. I was able to keep my seniority and generous time paid off. Then my journey began. This book grew from the journal I have kept along the way.

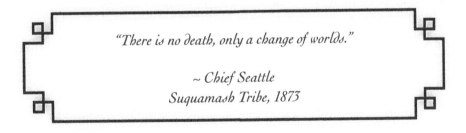

"There is no death, only a change of worlds."

~ Chief Seattle
Suquamash Tribe, 1873

CHAPTER 2

Jeff

12-5-1997

I had a special connection with Jeff. He felt very familiar to me as though we might have had a past life together. Jeff was 6' tall with wavy, brown hair that was streaked with gray. He was only 64-years-old and his slim, athletic body was now riddled with cancer. I thought to myself that this one was going to be hard because I was referring to his impending death that the doctor said could be within two months. His cancer was metastatic and I suspected that the cancer had spread to his brain due to his increasing confusion with each passing day.

One day his wife, Jean, was transferring him to bed and his right leg snapped which caused it to turn and face backward. He was in great pain while she called 911. The ambulance arrived shortly afterward and whisked him away to the nearest hospital.

The surgery went well and two weeks later, Jeff was sent home to their new apartment. It was in the retirement community of their dreams that they just moved into several months earlier. I was sitting with his wife and waiting for his anticipated homecoming. The van transportation people gently lifted him from the stretcher onto the adjustable hospital bed that hospice had provided. The Christmas tree, with all its twinkling lights, was placed near the foot of his bed. Jeff smiled as he gazed up at his special angel that topped the Douglas Fir.

I greeted Jeff with a hug and kiss on his forehead. I completed my nursing visit by taking his vital signs and assessing his lung sounds. I reviewed all of his medications with his caregiver and wife who were present and I answered their questions. I reinforced that they should call hospice if there were any problems.

Jeff continued to decline in spite of all the love that surrounded him. The family had plenty of morphine available and I reassured them that they could medicate him every two hours, if needed, per the instructions on the bottle. He slept most of the day when we were able to control his pain which was a blessing for his wife and caregivers.

His wife told me that she heard him saying, "I need to get my keys and I want my white pants. We have to wait in the dormitory for a while before we go home." His words did not surprise me because patients would frequently have deathbed visions while they processed their transition. Patients would also report seeing loved ones who already crossed to the other side. This was true for Jeff as he saw his wife's deceased mother whom he loved very much. This vision brought him and his wife great comfort.

I sensed his death was imminent due to the changes I saw in his condition - such as withdrawal from his surroundings and a decrease in his intake of food and liquids. His breathing was becoming more labored, but he seemed relatively peaceful. I made my nursing visits on a daily basis as well as frequent phone calls. I kissed him on the forehead and told him good-bye with a great heaviness in my heart. I had a premonition this would be the last time I would see him alive.

12-6-1997

When I called Jean in the morning, I told her I had a feeling that Jeff would die today. She repeated what I said and tried to absorb it all. Her next words were, "There are tears streaming down Jeff's face." After offering some words of comfort, I reassured her that I would call her around 3:00 p.m. to check on his condition. When I called Jean later that afternoon, she reported, "He is slipping away fast." Then, she exclaimed, "Oh, my God – he stopped breathing. I think he's gone."

I rushed over to their home and was greeted by Jeff's two daughters, his wife and two close friends. We all cried and hugged one another. Jean told me that in the morning his eyes had taken on a bright look with his pupils fully dilated. He had a look of amazement and joy that she had never seen before. He also appeared to be conversing with someone other than those present in the room.

Jean's spiritual friend, Jamie, was with her at the time of Jeff's death. At the moment of his death, Jamie saw a beautiful white light surrounding him. She gently said, "He just crossed over," while witnessing the release of his soul from his body. Jamie told me that she felt the presence of angels surrounding all of them, bringing peace and joy to Jeff as he made his transition. I remembered thinking that I wanted to be able to feel the presence of angels in my own life and I was in awe that Jamie seemed to be connected to higher realms. I was so grateful that she was there to help Jean cope with Jeff's transition.

One of the joys of being a hospice nurse is the inner knowing that I made a huge difference to patients and their families with the support and knowledge that I shared with them. I was so grateful for the support of the friends and families of my patients when death approached them. These individuals are like messengers and helpers from God and we are here on this earthly plane to help one another during the most difficult times - providing love, support and caring.

We are never alone. It is only our thoughts that make it seem so. Our belief in separation from the divine caused anguish in our lives. I knew that Jeff was happy now and free from pain.

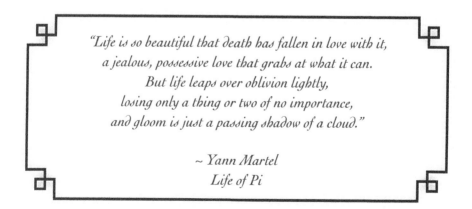

"Life is so beautiful that death has fallen in love with it,
a jealous, possessive love that grabs at what it can.
But life leaps over oblivion lightly,
losing only a thing or two of no importance,
and gloom is just a passing shadow of a cloud."

~ Yann Martel
Life of Pi

CHAPTER 3

Dennis

2-14-2007

I had a new patient who came on hospice service on a rainy Friday night. Dennis had beautiful blue eyes and he loved to wink at me when I approached him with my blood pressure cuff. He was a young 67-year-old with lung cancer that had spread to other organs of his body. His wife and sons were delightful and I enjoyed my interaction with them as we had many laughs together amid their impending loss.

I instructed the family how to give a few drops of liquid morphine under the tongue to manage his pain. I demonstrated how to help him get out of his chair by using two people on each side with their arms under his armpits to lift him up. I showed them how to reposition Dennis on his hospital bed, using pillows between his knees and ankles while he was lying on his side to prevent pressure sores.

I did not have much conversation with Dennis because he was very weak. He was such a brave fighter and refused to lie in the hospital bed we provided. He insisted on sitting in his recliner in the living room where he was present with his family. Much to our amazement, he was also able to gather up the strength to walk to the bathroom.

During the two weeks of his hospice service, I had the great honor of performing Reiki energy work on him. I sensed his relaxation and peace during the Reiki treatment. That energy was a part of me, too, because I was a channel for this beautiful light that came through me into another. Dennis' family was delighted that he was able to receive this gift because they witnessed the positive effect it had on him.

Dennis made his transition peacefully on a Saturday night with his beloved family at his bedside. I received the news through our hospice voicemail system and, later that morning, I saw his widow and family having breakfast at one of my favorite restaurants, Lazy Dog Cafe. I greeted them all with hugs, tears and condolences. We reminisced about what an incredible guy Dennis was and his sons talked about how grateful they were to have him for a dad.

Later that day, I went to my favorite park where I treasure the peace and solitude. As I sat there watching the tree limbs dance with the wind, I reflected on all the hospice patients I had recently lost and felt the sadness and grief of losing them. When I looked at the trees, I saw a swarm of butterflies flying around. There was this one butterfly, black with beige edges, that kept circling my head. I thought it was very strange and asked, "Is that you, Dennis? If it is, you can let me know by landing on my hand." A minute later, the same butterfly brushed against my forehead; landed on my hand; and stayed there for two minutes. I was mesmerized by this experience and knew that Dennis came to me in this form to let me know that all was well. His message from the afterlife was powerful for me. That magical experience helped birth the title of this book.

The next day, I had my appointment with my massage therapist who was truly gifted with psychic abilities. I told her the story about Dennis, which she loved. She had her hands on my back and said, "Mary, what was the name of that patient?" I told her it was Dennis and she replied, "He's here now. He wants you to know how happy he is. He is having fun visiting the significant people and places that had meaning for him and his family." She went on to say that we had a real soul connection that I was not aware of but never doubted. She expressed that we had a spiritual agreement that I would be there for him and his family when he crossed over beyond the veil.

I attended Dennis's funeral five days after that experience. During the reception, I saw his wife's friend, Joanne, sitting at a table with a group of women. I told them the butterfly story and one of Joanne's friends responded, "I have a similar story. About five days after

Dennis passed, a blue bird landed on our patio and kept pecking at our sliding door. He stayed there a very long time and kept up the pecking until my husband went upstairs to get our digital camera. He took a picture of the blue bird and transposed it over a picture of Dennis." That picture was at the memorial service. It showed Dennis with his outstretched arm holding the bird in his palm.

Death is nothing at all. It does not count. I have only slipped away into the next room. Nothing has happened. Everything remains exactly as it was. I am I, and you are you, and the old life that we lived so fondly together is untouched, unchanged. Whatever we were to each other, that we are still. Call me by the old familiar name. Speak of me in the easy way which you always used. Put no difference into your tone. Wear no forced air of solemnity or sorrow. Laugh as we always laughed at the little jokes that we enjoyed together. Play, smile, think of me, pray for me. Let my name be ever the household word that it always was. Let it be spoken without an effort, without the ghost of a shadow upon it. Life means all that it ever meant. It is the same as it ever was. There is absolute and unbroken continuity. What is this death but a negligible accident? Why should I be out of mind because I am out of sight? I am but waiting for you, for an interval, somewhere very near, just round the corner. All is well. Nothing is hurt; nothing is lost. One brief moment and all will be as it was before. How we shall laugh at the trouble of parting when we meet again!

~ Henry Scott Holland
Death Is Nothing at All

CHAPTER 4

6-12-2007

One of my very favorite patients was Lil, a spry 94-year-old with a humped back. She was 4' 8" tall and wore thick glasses. Having lost 95% of her vision, she was nearly blind with macular degeneration. She was so cute and an absolute sweetheart; she was the grandmother I never had and I loved her dearly. I visited her twice a week as she was on service for cardiac disease.

Lil had a great sense of humor and she even dressed up as Charlie Chaplin on Halloween. She also loved to share stories about her life; particularly her party-filled youth. She told me about the time she had mistakenly made a date with two different men for a particular Saturday night. They both showed up at her door within minutes of each other and she had to choose between the two of them. She treasured reflecting about her many love relationships with interesting men.

Lil lived in subsidized housing. She did not have much in the way of material possessions, but she was rich with love. People loved her – especially the people who managed the building. Lil was their favorite. I was friendly with the managers and we laughed a lot during my visits with her.

Lil didn't want to be in a nursing home and wanted to stay in her own place. I told her I would do my best to try and make that happen because I knew it was important to her. I remembered when she was getting close to dying and I sat at her feet and cried. She stroked my head and recited this poem:

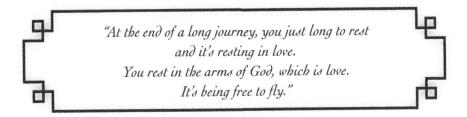

"At the end of a long journey, you just long to rest
and it's resting in love.
You rest in the arms of God, which is love.
It's being free to fly."

I made sure Lil had plenty of morphine at her bedside and that she was as comfortable as possible so she could remain in her little senior apartment that she absolutely loved. She had lived there for the past 25 years and all of the people in her life loved her bright spirit and infectious laughter. On one of my last visits, I started to cry when I thought about losing her because the signs were there: increased weakness, lack of appetite and withdrawal from the world.

Lil took half an Ativan with Ibuprofen to go to sleep. Her back was curved and she was in constant pain. I believed that cannabis would have helped her. Of course, she would have had to take it in edible form because she could not smoke. She had chronic obstructive pulmonary disease and she was on oxygen most of the time. I never gave her a hard time about the oxygen as she knew when she needed it. If she wanted to be off the oxygen for a while, I would let her do what she wanted because that was my style of nursing. I was not the expert on her life and she knew her body.

My precious Lil was dying before my eyes and my heart was breaking. She had been on hospice service for two years and I looked forward to my visit with her each week. She lost her son to heart disease three years ago and she also lost a sister many years before that. She was looking forward to being reunited with them on the other side.

Lil was a very spiritual lady and we talked about spiritual experiences on many occasions. One time she told me about a vision she had shortly after her sister died at a young age. Her sister appeared before her in a white, glowing gown and there was light all around her. Her sister told Lil not to grieve because she was very happy and someday she would be there when it was Lil's time to cross over.

Lil mentioned that she sensed a presence coming toward her lately and she thought it might be her mother and that gave her great peace. She told me many times that she was ready to die and was not afraid. She talked about her belief in life after death and knew it would be glorious. However, she was concerned about her surviving son and the effect her death would have on him because she was his last living family member.

Lil also shared with me that she saw this vision of her deceased brother with a little boy and they were sitting at the edge of her bed. She could actually see them. They would come to visit her and I knew they brought her comfort. Lil said they were her guardian angels and I believed her when she told me all those things. That was why I was her nurse. Since she was so spiritual, she had this ability to see spirits and that was what we all were – spirits having a human experience that live forever.

Lil and I talked about end-of-life issues. She said she was grateful for the life she had lived and had no regrets. She told me she loved me and looked forward to my visits. I told her I loved her, too, and would miss her dearly. We hugged and cried together. I asked her to give me a sign from the other side that she was happy and okay and she agreed to do that.

One of the best lessons I ever received was from Lil. She told me that she had a son who had died in his late 50s. She said, "You know, Mary, it's like he never died because I feel him around me all the time. It's good, so I don't think of him as being dead because he's here with me." When she said that, I thought, "How cool is that?" I also have two boys and it really bothered me to think of losing one of them. However, I knew that they would be around me because all I would have to do is think of them to make that connection. So, I thought about my son who lived in Chicago. All I needed to be was love and connect with him in the energy of love. The more I went to that place of love, the better my life worked.

I had been running from death all of my life. It was strange that I would be a hospice nurse and be running from death, but the running away was my own fears and not being able to face them. But, death happens to us all.

6-25-2007

Today was a bad day for Lil. We had to get an electric, adjustable hospital bed for her and that made her more comfortable. It was difficult to see her lying in bed at 3:00 p.m. when she was usually sitting in her recliner watching her favorite TV show, *Judge Judy*. We had our continuous care team of nurses and personal care aides at her bedside to care for her in the remaining hours or days. I kissed her forehead and told her I loved her. She said, "I love you, too," and managed to squeeze my hand.

When Lil started to decline fast, I would not let myself think of her approaching death. I felt myself pull away from her emotionally because I knew the pain of losing her would be great. She did not want to be in a nursing home and be totally blind. I assured her she would not go blind, but I was unsure about the nursing home part because she lived alone. I was delighted that the interdisciplinary team made the decision to keep her at home with continuous care. Her 70-year-old newlywed son and his bride had no intention of caring for her and neither were they capable.

6-26-2007

Lil died today. I received the call on my cell phone from the nurse who was with her these past few days because it was my day off. I had thoughts about going over to see Lil this morning but decided against doing that. I felt so sad that I would not be seeing her anymore and was crying on and off throughout the day. I felt honored and privileged to had known her and to have had the close relationship we shared. I treasured the many wonderful hours of listening to her stories and laughing at her antics. I missed her dearly already.

As I am writing this, I feel a sense of remorse that I was not at

Lil's bedside when she made her transition. I knew in Lil's higher consciousness that there was nothing to forgive because I did what I needed to do to protect myself from the pain. There had been so many losses, but there was true gain for the one who made his or her transition. I know Lil forgives me for not being there when she died because everything is of divine right order. I knew that I was not ready to lose her. I believe that Lil's sister came to her when Lil was nearing her transition and that brings me great comfort. I know she is resting in the arms of God.

7-3-2007

Today was a warm, sunny afternoon and I was thinking about Lil. I was between nursing visits and I had to pull over to check my trunk for supplies that I needed for my next nursing visit. I was going through my medical supply box which I had done dozens of times in the past six months. Then, I spotted Lil's Christmas card among the catheters and dressings. The envelope had a very large inscription, "To Mary," with a wink. I opened the white envelope to read her classic handwriting, "Merry Christmas. Love, Lil." It was a huge "Wow" moment and I stood there motionless. The card and the envelope did not have a wrinkle or mark on it, which was truly amazing considering all the times that I had been in that box rearranging the supplies. I believed it was a sign from Lil that I had asked for, because as I have said, I had been through this box several times and never saw the card or envelope. It was truly her message to me as I felt her presence and love surrounding me.

There was a memorial service for her at the senior housing complex where she lived. I attended it as well as many of the tenants who also loved her. We all held helium balloons as we shared our favorite memories about her. Then we all released the balloons. They flew away fast except for the one I was holding that got caught up in the branches of a tree for the longest time. It was as if Lil was reluctant to leave us. We all shouted, "Go! It's okay to go now!" After about 30 seconds, the balloon set itself free from the branches and flew away. I had the distinct feeling that I was the one that Lil was reluctant to leave behind and now she was free to fly just like the poem she recited to me.

Lil's son told me to take whatever memorabilia I wanted from Lil's apartment. I chose a white butterfly ornament that I have hanging from the rearview mirror of my car. I often touch that ornament when I am stopped at a light, remembering Lil's sweet smile. I still feel that special connection to her.

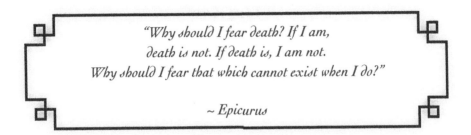

"Why should I fear death? If I am,
death is not. If death is, I am not.
Why should I fear that which cannot exist when I do?"

~ Epicurus

CHAPTER 5

Walt

———— ❋ ————

7-6-2007

I called this morning to check in with Ann, the stepmom of my 29-year-old patient, Walt, who had testicular cancer. He was blond, tall and thin with an adorable smile that I occasionally got to witness. He lived in a small two-bedroom apartment with his dad and stepmom. His bedroom was filled with posters from his favorite rock bands as well as sports memorabilia.

Walt was withdrawn when I made nursing visits to him. I joked with him, but rarely got a smile. Lately, he was feeling depressed because a group of his close friends were going to come to visit him and they all decided to back out the morning of the visit. I felt so bad for him.

I had witnessed Walt's journey through the various stages of the dying process during the months he had been on hospice service. I had recently read Dr. Elisabeth Kubler-Ross's book *On Death and Dying*. She outlined the stages as the following: first stage was denial and isolation; second stage was anger; third stage was bargaining; fourth stage was depression; and the final stage was acceptance. In her book, she stated that it was very common for patients to vacillate between all of these stages before reaching the acceptance stage. Fortunately, Walt had reached the final stage of acceptance in the past few days.

During our phone conversation, Ann said that Walt was about the same. I was still on the phone with her when I heard him call out,

"Help me. I can't breathe." I told Ann to give him morphine and said that I would be right over. When I got there, he had already passed, which she was not aware of. Most likely, Walt died of a blood clot to the lungs.

Ann called Walt's dad and he came right over. It was difficult to witness Walt's dad sobbing as he held his son in his arms for the last time. I made the required call to hospice to report the death and requested a spiritual counselor. The spiritual counselor came to help all of us. Walt's passing affected me so deeply that I was crying, too. This was especially hard because it had only been less than two weeks since Lil died. It was so difficult to be a hospice nurse at times like these.

Sometimes, I thought about working in the newborn nursery. But then again, I knew that I was right where I was supposed to be. Someone once told me that making your transition is the best thing that can happen to you. It was hard to wrap my head around that when someone like Walt died at a young age.

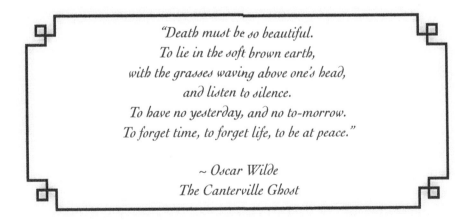

"Death must be so beautiful.
To lie in the soft brown earth,
with the grasses waving above one's head,
and listen to silence.
To have no yesterday, and no to-morrow.
To forget time, to forget life, to be at peace."

~ Oscar Wilde
The Canterville Ghost

CHAPTER 6

Pamela

~ ❋ ~

8-6-2007

Pamela was a 36-year-old African-American female with aggressive gastric cancer. She wore her curly black hair in a ponytail and continued to put on makeup which lifted her spirits. She was living with her sister in a small, two-bedroom apartment and had a rebellious 14-year-old son, Jason, who lived with his dad in Michigan. She loved her son very much and felt sad that he was not in her life since the divorce.

In spite of her terminal diagnosis, she was positive and upbeat when I came to visit her. Her stomach was huge from the tumor and she could no longer take care of herself. Her pain had been well-managed with round-the-clock morphine, but she started having multiple seizures due to the high morphine doses. The doctor ordered anti-seizure medications, but that did not seem to help much. We finally got her into an electric hospital bed and it was put in the small living room.

During my visits with Pamela, she talked about her feelings regarding her terminal illness and her impending death. She was grateful to share this with me because her family was not comfortable talking about the dying process. They would change the subject and try to cheer her up. According to Dr. Elisabeth Kubler-Ross, "It might be helpful if more people would talk about death and dying as an intrinsic part of life just as they do not hesitate to mention when

18

someone is expecting a new baby." I was comfortable talking about death and dying because I knew how beneficial it was for patients to express their deepest emotions and fears.

Pamela's family was frantically trying to get her son, Jason, to her bedside before she died. They were able to arrange an airline flight for him the next morning. Unfortunately, he arrived five hours after she passed peacefully in her sleep.

I visited Jason at the apartment a few days later and he looked sad and broken. We talked about his mom and the impact she had on his life. He said he felt sad that he did not get to see her before she made her transition. I gave him a warm hug and handed him some spiritual poems about death and dying. I felt it might be helpful for him to have inspirational literature when he was ready to read it.

Helping my patient's family deal with the terminal process and the emotional issues that would come up along the way was a huge part of my role as a hospice nurse. Typically, this was the role the social worker had; but as the nurse who visited frequently, I was the person who they would connect with. I was happy to be there for them in their time of need.

This is my favorite quote about death from *The Prophet* by Kahlil Gibran:

"You would know the secret of death.
But how shall you find it unless you seek it in the heart of life?
The owl whose night-bound eyes are blind unto the day
cannot unveil the mystery of light.
If you would indeed behold the spirit of death,
open your heart wide unto the body of life.
For life and death are one, even as the river and the sea are one.

In the depth of your hopes and desires lies your silent knowledge of the beyond;
And like seeds dreaming beneath the snow your heart dreams of spring.
Trust the dreams, for in them is hidden the gate to eternity.
Your fear of death is but the trembling of the shepherd when he stands
before the king whose hand is to be laid upon him in honour.
Is the shepherd not joyful beneath his trembling,
that he shall wear the mark of the king?
Yet is he not more mindful of his trembling?

For what is it to die but to stand naked in the wind and to melt into the sun?
And what is it to cease breathing, but to free the breath from its restless tides,
that it may rise and expand and seek God unencumbered?

Only when you drink from the river of silence shall you indeed sing.
And when you have reached the mountain top, then you shall begin to climb.
And when the earth shall claim your limbs, then shall you truly dance."

CHAPTER 7

Lillie

~ ❋ ~

12-19-2007

I attended the funeral of Lillie, who was 90-years-old with Alzheimer's. She had been on hospice service for two-and-a-half-years. I became very close friends with her daughter-in-law, Joyce, who lovingly took care of Lillie day and night for three years. Joyce and I used to sit on the patio and talk over a cup of tea during my nursing visits. I remember thinking how blessed I was to be paid for work that I loved and the wonderful people I became friends with.

The day before she died, I went to the nursing home where Lillie had been for the past seven days on respite care. Joyce was at Lillie's bedside and was in deep denial that Lillie was very close to dying. Joyce wanted to move Lillie back to their apartment where she had cared for her because she wanted Lillie to die at home. However, Lillie's daughter, Jessica, was a Registered Nurse and the durable power of attorney for health care. Jessica made the decision that it would be too difficult for Lillie to be transported back to Joyce and Bob's home. Joyce had to accept that decision. She truly wanted what was best for Lillie and I spent much of my nursing visit talking to Joyce about the peace that comes with acceptance.

Lillie died on my birthday, December 14th, which was my day off. I called Joyce the night before to request that she call me when Lillie passed away so I could be there for her and Bob, Lillie's son. Joyce did not call me when Lillie died in the early morning hour at the nursing home. The on-call nurse was called to assist with Lillie's passing and comfort the family.

I felt fortunate that I was able to be of service to Joyce at that difficult time of letting go. I was extremely grateful that I saw Lillie and gave her my last good-bye kiss the day before she made her transition. Letting go of our loved ones is never easy. But, the love never dies.

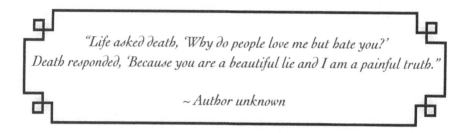

"Life asked death, 'Why do people love me but hate you?'
Death responded, 'Because you are a beautiful lie and I am a painful truth."

~ Author unknown

CHAPTER 8

Emily

~ ✿ ~

3-15-2008

I made a visit to my amazing patient, Emily, with my nursing supervisor who had to evaluate my job performance. Emily's 22-year-old son, Mike, was present for the visit and was feeling very stressed about his mother's declining health. He was in deep denial about his mother's terminal illness and had frequent angry outbursts.

Mike and I talked about having honest and open communication with his mother about the dying process. I educated him about the dying process and the care required for his mom during her terminal disease. He acknowledged that he had been avoiding that conversation with her and set an intention to talk to her about her feelings. "When anger, resentment, and guilt can be worked through, the family will then go through a phase of preparatory grief, just as the dying person does. The more this grief can be expressed before death, the less unbearable it becomes afterward," (Kubler-Ross). His anxiety level diminished during our conversation and the remainder of the visit went smoothly. As my supervisor and I left their home, she said to me, "You are a great nurse, but I don't know how you can do this every day." I replied, "I don't know how I do this either."

I purchased Deepak Chopra's book, *Power, Freedom and Grace,* and read it to Emily. She loved the few pages on what happens when we die, so I gave her the book. Mike would read to her in her times of distress and it calmed her down so much. I also gave her the music

CD *Grace* by Snatam Kaur and she played it over and over. This CD was my favorite because the spiritual lyrics spoke to me of God's love and about our eternal soul - which was one with God.

Sweet Emily was two years older than I and she was such a vibrant being in her youth. Emily had beautiful red hair that was halfway down her back that she wore in a ponytail. She had a joyful laugh that wrinkled her nose. She was spiritual and loved to talk about the meaning of life and death. She gave so much to others in service work and she enjoyed that it filled her soul.

I knew Emily would be a hard one to lose. The loss can be so great at times. Even though I know they are going to a place of bliss, I cannot help thinking of how I will miss their presence in my life. I cannot get over the level of love and devotion from the family members at the time of farewell and the final good-bye kiss. My heart breaks for the pain I witness with this huge loss in their lives, yet, I know what a tremendous difference I make to the family and the patients. They all feel the love I bring along with my nursing visits. Long hugs are so comforting for all of us. Love is all that matters.

I can't even begin to count all the deaths I have seen over the past years. When there is no life left in the body, where does that energy go? The body is a temporary shell that houses our soul for a short period of time. There is no doubt in my mind that we go on to a greater experience of being. There should be great joy in the transition period between this earthly life and the next place of bliss.

Unfortunately, we want to own and possess the people in our lives because we are so fearful of being alone. The reality is that we are never alone because we are a part of the great I AM. We were never born and we will never die. I always write on our hospice condolence card to the families, "Love never dies". Because we are love, we never die and neither do our loved ones. We simply have a short period of not being able to connect and communicate like we used to. "Nothing happens to us when we die," writes Deepak Chopra and I find that very comforting.

"It is the secret of the world that all things subsist and do not die,
but retire a little from sight and afterwards return again."

~ Ralph Waldo Emerson
Essays: Second Series

CHAPTER 9

Rosemary

---※---

6-5-2008

Rosemary was the patient I had the most fun with! It was always a delightful visit because she was jovial and witty. She was a 52-year-old lesbian with cervical cancer that had spread. Rosemary was roughly 100 pounds overweight, in spite of the cancer, and her partner, Jill, was as thin as a rail. They were Buddhist and tried to convert me. I told them that my religion was love and I was comfortable with the chanting and the artifacts as I am a spiritual person instead of a religious woman.

I was convinced that the group that came every Saturday morning to participate in three to four hours of chanting kept Rosemary alive longer than the hospice doctors imagined. We had fun because we all sat on Rosemary's bed and they sang a song to me that Jill wrote. The song was about a flood and a guy who floated to safety due to hanging on to his girlfriend's large breasts that acted as life preservers. We laughed until our sides ached! It was so much fun knowing them, but there was always the pain of losing the patients and their loved ones.

Rosemary was a real maverick and smoked cannabis during my visits. She was comfortable in her own skin and I admired that, but I had to fight the prejudice I felt about her excessive weight. She was also a gifted singer and songwriter. She produced a CD of her music and gifted it to me during one of my many visits. I often played that

CD in my car as I was traveling back home at the end of my workday and some of the songs moved me to tears.

When my territory got changed closer to my home, I had to give up the patients that I serviced in my old territory. Rosemary wanted me to stay on as her nurse, so I requested to keep her even though she lived 26 miles away. Luckily, my request was granted and it was worth the extra miles just to keep her as my patient. I truly loved her.

My husband and I were invited to a holiday party at their home. It was one of the best parties we attended because of their interesting spiritual friends. It was a joy to have meaningful conversations with like-minded people. I felt happy and grateful that I was able to attend Rosemary's last Christmas party. Unfortunately, Rosemary was too weak to enjoy the party and remained in bed watching Christmas movies.

Jill was in deep denial that Rosemary was terminal. She bought Rosemary a bike two months ago for her birthday. She kept talking about the two of them going away to Santa Barbara for a romantic weekend, even though Rosemary did not have the strength to get out of bed. She refused to talk to Rosemary about her emotions and feelings, which was distressful for Rosemary. "If members of a family can share these emotions together, they will gradually face the reality of impending separation and come to an acceptance of it together. The most heartbreaking time, perhaps, for the family is the final phase, when the patient is slowly detaching himself from his world including his family" (Kubler-Ross). It was expected that Rosemary would die within two months.

My husband and I attended Rosemary's memorial service and the place was filled with her Buddhist friends chanting a mantra for 30 minutes. Rosemary's dad sat in the aisle in front of us. He did not approve of his daughter's spiritual path and appeared uncomfortable with it all. My heart broke for the pain I witnessed in his eyes. Previously, he had lost his only son four years before and now he was saying farewell to his last surviving child.

Two weeks after Rosemary's passing, my husband and I were sitting on a patio overlooking the Pacific Ocean. We were reminiscing about her when Gary looked up at the clouds and said, "Look at that angel cloud above us. Rosemary has come back to tell you that all is well and she is with the angels." I got chills all over my body and I knew his statement was true. I looked up at that angel cloud and felt the joyful presence of Rosemary.

I tried to keep in touch with Jill after Rosemary made her transition and she didn't return my calls. I felt that it was too painful for her to keep that connection with me. It was another lesson about letting go. It reminded me of a saying – People are in your life for a reason, a season or a lifetime. I was in their life for a reason and a season.

For Christmas one year, Rosemary gave me a lovely candleholder that has three tiers on a brushed nickel base. I use that candleholder every day during my spiritual practice. I think of Rosemary whenever I light a candle and I am grateful that I was her nurse during her last days on earth.

In the years I have been a hospice registered nurse, I have witnessed tremendous spiritual growth within myself. I cannot possibly watch all those people die and not know there is something more than we are privy to on this earthly plane. A frequent thought I had was, "If it happens to everyone, then it can't be that bad."

I have learned so much from my patients – how to live well and how to die. I marvel at the incredible family members who gave up their lives for a dying loved one. But, death is just an illusion. I believe we leave the body to become free spirits melding in the bliss of God's love. If everyone could grasp this, it would be much easier to let our loved ones go on to that blissful state of being.

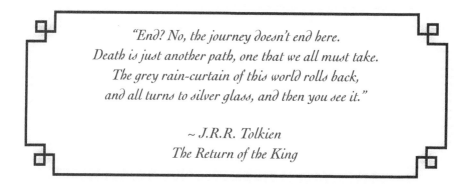

"End? No, the journey doesn't end here.
Death is just another path, one that we all must take.
The grey rain-curtain of this world rolls back,
and all turns to silver glass, and then you see it."

~ J.R.R. Tolkien
The Return of the King

CHAPTER 10

Carolyn

7-8-2008

One of my most challenging patients was Carolyn who was 65-years-old and had so much illness that it was a wonder she was alive. She had respiratory problems that required her to continuously be on oxygen at 10 liters per minute. The normal range for oxygen delivery was two to three liters per minute. She also had an immune deficiency that kept her at risk for infections. She was bedbound. When she had a urinary catheter, she had frequent urinary infections. The doctor decided to discontinue the catheter due to the infections and she also had to wear adult diapers.

After taking her vitals and conversing with her daughter, I gave Carolyn Reiki. She told me, "I have never felt this good in my life." Her mind was sharp, but her body had failed her. I felt so blessed to have the ability to make a profound difference in her life. Carolyn's condition had stabilized in the three months I had been doing Reiki on her. I have had many patients' pain diminish, as well as anxiety and depression, after performing Reiki on them.

Carolyn told me that the first time I walked into her bedroom for my nursing visit, she saw a bright aura around my body and thought, "This one is going to be interesting." She had several nurses before me due to the change in staff and nursing territories. She was on hospice service for two years before I became her nurse.

Her daughter, Laurie, was her 24-hour caregiver who slept in her mother's bedroom with her. Carolyn's husband, who was 17 years her junior, slept in the guest bedroom. I saw the stress on Laurie's face when I made my visits. The two of them were very enmeshed. I encouraged Laurie to take care of herself by going to the beach for an afternoon or having lunch with a friend. I also suggested a caregiver support group that would help her deal with the stress of her mother's care. She never took my advice. It was so important for caregivers to take extra good care of themselves so that they had more to give to their loved ones. It was just like the flight attendants that would tell us to put on our oxygen mask first before assisting others.

Two weeks ago, Laurie decided to get a pet ferret for her daughter, Lisa. Lisa really wanted a kitten. Laurie told me they had cats previously that got hit by cars and decided to try something different. The ferret loved to come into the bedroom when I made my nursing visits to Carolyn. One day, the ferret decided to crawl up my leg while I was taking Carolyn's blood pressure. I screamed and that brought Laurie running into the room. We all had a great laugh about it, but afterward, I made sure Carolyn's door was closed when I had my nursing visits.

Carolyn and I used to discuss life after death during our time together. She had many spiritual gifts and loved our spiritual talks. I asked her if she would give me a sign that she was happy and well after she crossed over. She thought that was a great idea and decided the sign would be yellow flowers.

Several months after Carolyn passed, I was riding my bike along the ocean path when I saw a long string of yellow flowers lining the bike path. I got chills all over my body and felt Carolyn's presence and joy. I thanked her for the afterlife message of the gift of yellow flowers and that all was well.

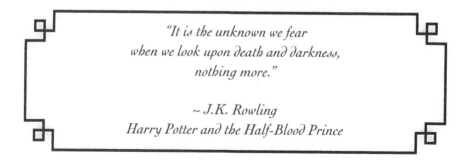

*"It is the unknown we fear
when we look upon death and darkness,
nothing more."*

*~ J.K. Rowling
Harry Potter and the Half-Blood Prince*

CHAPTER 11

Ngoc

~ ❋ ~

8-19-2008

Even though I was off duty for a five-day weekend, my alpha pager was beeping in the car and telling me that my Vietnamese patient, Ngoc, had a change of condition. I had to call the office and tell them I was off for the weekend so they would get someone there. A few days before, her family was telling me, "She's telling crazy stories about being pregnant and giving birth and now she is looking for the baby." I told them that I felt that a new baby signified new life and that she was giving birth to that new life.

Ngoc was such a sweetheart! She was so gentle and kind and she was the mother of 14 children. Her English was poor, but we found ways to communicate. She loved it when I kissed her forehead every visit and caressed her arm. She told me she loved me and I told her I loved her, too. I also loved her family and I was able to know so many of them. They loved their mom and it was an honor to care for her.

I was impressed with this family. I remember going to Ngoc's home to admit her to our hospice program one Saturday evening because I was on call. I was not happy that I had to make a late visit that night, but then I met four of her kids and felt their wonderful energy of love and commitment. My resentment about making that visit disappeared.

I felt a wash of sadness coming over me because we were losing her. I would lose her and her lovely family. Sometimes, I wondered how I had the courage to face all those losses in my life. Knowing that I made a huge difference in the lives I touched enabled me to keep doing what I was doing. My work made me realize how precious life was and the importance of the people in our lives because tomorrow was promised to no one.

11-6-2008

Even though Ngoc had 14 children, it was her eight daughters that were present for all my visits. Perhaps it was in a woman's DNA to be the nurturer. In all my years of hospice, I noticed how it was usually the women who were present for the caregiving and dying process. Rarely did I see the sons present, and if they were, their visits were very short.

Ngoc's daughters had been trying to help their father accept the fact that his wife was dying. He had been in constant denial and wanted to send her back to the hospital. While in the hospital, Ngoc had shared with one of her daughters that she did not want any more painful, aggressive treatments and that she wanted to be at home and die in her own bed surrounded by family. "The unwavering focus on treatments for sustaining life can leave someone who is living with an advanced disease physically uncomfortable, feeling lost and confused, not knowing how to get through each day or how to plan for the future," states Ira Byock, MD in his book *The Best Care Possible*.

Her daughters asked me to tell their father about his wife's condition and they would translate what I said. I told him we couldn't send her back to the hospital because she was dying. The best place for her was to be in her home surrounded by the people who loved her. He asked if the doctors could fix her and I explained that if there was something that they could have done about her cancer, they would have done it. I shared with him that she wanted to be free of her diseased body and sought to go home to God. She would be able to do that much easier if he told her it was okay for her to go.

I expressed to him that she would be free of the pain and would be surrounded in love and bliss. I gently confided that he would not

32

need to worry because his wife would be waiting for him on the other side to help him cross over when it was his time – just as he would do for their children when it was their turn to go home and be with God.

There was a very long silence before he said, "I want to die with her. Can you help me do it?" I started crying at that point because I felt his pain of losing the woman who had been by his side for 62 years. I told him that the soul would decide when it was ready to leave this planet and that I would not "play God" and assist with his death because of the pain he was feeling. Then he asked me if I would continue to see her and I reassured him that I would.

For the past two weeks, Ngoc had been talking about the newborn baby and how she needed to find it because it was dying. She would get out of bed at night looking for the baby, so her daughters decided to buy her a doll that talked. When I would visit her, she would be holding the doll lovingly, stroking its forehead and talking about how they had to plan for the funeral because the baby was dead. I told her family that this was her way of processing her transition. Being a mom of 14 was where Ngoc's identity existed.

I called one of Ngoc's daughters on Friday to schedule a visit because she was declining fast. She told me her mom's breathing was more labored. They put her on oxygen so she would be more comfortable. The daughter said I could skip the visit, but I felt a strong urge to go to their home and she said to come by in the afternoon.

When I arrived, Ngoc was having an irregular breathing pattern, which is a classic end-of-life sign. I looked into Ngoc's eyes and saw such an amazing look of peace. Her face appeared luminous. I sensed the presence of angels as I sat there with her. I felt a beautiful stillness and a divine presence that filled the room. I cried as I kissed her forehead, knowing this was her last day on earth.

Her daughters were crying, too, because they were aware that the end was coming soon. There was a part of me that wanted to leave so they could have privacy with their mom. I ended up staying and sat in a chair at the end of her bed, observing the family and the grieving process.

Two minutes later, one daughter said, "Mary, she stopped breathing." I took out my stethoscope and I did not hear a heartbeat. I shook my head and said, "She's gone." Everyone started crying, hugging and comforting one another. I knew that she had waited until I arrived to take that last breath, so I would be present to comfort all of them – even though I needed comforting myself. I knew that I would miss this sweet little lady and her incredible daughters.

I had to miss Ngoc's funeral as I would be traveling to Sedona to get trained to be a Reiki Master. Fortunately, I was there for her transition to the bliss and love that I know awaits all of us on the other side. My job was well-done and her family thanked me for being there at the time of her passing. They expressed gratitude for all that I had done for their mother and I left their home with a feeling of love and gratitude that my sweet patient was free of pain and free to fly.

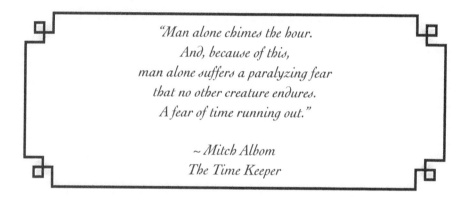

"Man alone chimes the hour.
And, because of this,
man alone suffers a paralyzing fear
that no other creature endures.
A fear of time running out."

~ Mitch Albom
The Time Keeper

CHAPTER 12

Loretta

~ ❖ ~

12-2-2008

One of the most interesting patients I ever had was Loretta. She knew she was dying and was fighting death. She kept running from it, propelling herself out of her chair with a strength that defied the fragile and frail 74-year-old body that was riddled with cancer. She was a character and I fell in love with her the first moment I met her. She went from one medical problem to another and I saw the fear mounting in her. She used these various problems to distract her from the realization that she was dying.

Loretta spent her last days creating havoc for her husband, Ralph, and her son, Jim, by refusing to sleep or sit still. One cool fall night, she propelled herself out of bed at 2:00 a.m. She ran out of the house in her pink nightgown, screaming to the neighbors that her husband wanted to kill her. Her embarrassed husband managed to wrestle her back into their home.

Ralph called me the next morning to say he could not handle being her caregiver 24/7. He was at his breaking point and needed to find an alternate plan. I contacted our hospice social worker, Vivian, and informed her about what had transpired. Vivian visited their home that afternoon. She found a suitable nursing home that was within seven miles of where they lived. After faxing over Loretta's medical records, the director of the nursing home reviewed it and accepted Loretta for admission.

We were able to put Loretta on hospice crisis care, which meant that hospice paid for her stay and daily visits. We warned the nursing staff that she was a runner! They took it lightly because she was so weak on admission and they probably did not think she had the strength to get out of bed. Loretta managed to escape the first night there, and apparently, no one saw her leave. The police found her walking the streets in her nightgown while yelling out foul language. Luckily, she had an identification bracelet. The police took her to the emergency room for an evaluation and then transported her back to the nursing home.

I made a visit at the nursing home the next day. Loretta's husband and son were there in her tiny room. I requested that Loretta's son and I talk in private. We had a very honest conversation about Loretta's past, which was something she never disclosed to any of the hospice workers during the initial hospice evaluation.

Her son stated that Loretta never forgave herself for causing her oldest daughter's estrangement. Loretta has two other children who had not seen her in three years. None of her children had visited her since she was admitted into our hospice service. All of them were aware of her terminal condition.

Loretta was not at peace with herself and the doctors wanted to throw more medicine into her. They did not realize that no amount of medication would soothe a tormented soul. In fact, some of the medications would cause more problems. I wondered whether it was too late for Loretta and her children to make amends and heal this wound that had been festering for quite some time.

I listened to her son, Jim, with great empathy. We talked about my own realization through the years of my hospice work: that we are not our bodies. Who we really are was whole, perfect and complete. We were part of that same energy that held all of the planets in line and made our blood circulate through our bodies. I knew I could not have done this work if I did not believe that we were all part of something much greater than what our human minds could grasp.

Loretta remained at that nursing home for five more days. I visited her regularly and spent most of my visit consoling her husband and son. During my last visit, they told me that they tried to get the rest of the family to visit Loretta, but they were unsuccessful. She died that very night. I felt sad for her family members who were unable to put the past behind them and to find love and forgiveness for Loretta. Forgiveness is the gift we give ourselves.

I witnessed fear in varying degrees in my patients, but Loretta's fear was huge. "Americans are scared to death of dying. And with good reason. While rarely easy under any circumstances, we make dying a lot harder than it has to be. Our society and mainstream American culture have never grappled with the fundamental fact of mortality: therefore, we do not know what to expect or what is possible." states Ira Byock, MD in his book *The Best Care Possible*.

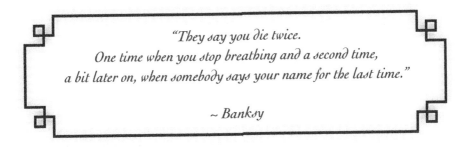

"They say you die twice.
One time when you stop breathing and a second time,
a bit later on, when somebody says your name for the last time."

~ Banksy

CHAPTER 13

Billie

~ ❋ ~

12-11-2008

Billie was a very special lady who turned 90-years-old a few months ago. She was almost 5' tall and had short, wavy, white hair. She had an amazing smile and deep blue eyes that would light up when I came in the room for my nursing visit. She cherished the attention I showered on her and loved it when I hugged and kissed her at the start and end of my weekly visit. She had a little terrier-mix dog that slept in her bed and was very protective. Her dog tolerated my presence and watched my every move.

Billie loved to tell stories about her youth during World War II. She knew famous movie stars and politicians and enjoyed sharing about her relationships with them. She loved people and possessed a degree in Psychology. She appeared larger than life and was so strong, just like myself, and that was why we related so well to each other.

We talked about life after death as she knew she was an immortal soul. Billie was convinced that she would die in February because that was when all the significant people in her life had passed on. I asked if she would contact me after her death and she agreed she would. I could not bear to think about the day that she would make her final transition.

I saw Billie two days before she died and she was unresponsive but appeared comfortable. She loved when I gave her Reiki treatments every time I saw her and the intensity had grown through our sessions. She felt the warmth and vibration because she was so open.

I proceeded to do a Reiki treatment on her using the symbol that helped in crossing over to the other side called Happy Trails. I sensed that she knew I was there and felt my tears. I brought the CD by *Deva Primal and Mitten*. The song called "Soul in Wonder" is about our passage from this existence to the next. I played it for her that last day. On my way home, I drove to my favorite beach, Crystal Cove. I walked on the beach and sensed that Billie was there. She said to me, "Enjoy your life, Mary."

When Billie was dying, the company sent another nurse to the death visit. I was somewhat relieved because it was so difficult to lose her. Her spirit was so vibrant and indomitable that I could not imagine her dying, but it was her time. There was a huge part of me that would run away from death and I was happy to run that day. I am sure she was smiling on the day she made her transition because she was ready. No one can escape death; no matter how rich and/or famous they are.

I do shamanic energy healing work in a special room in my modest home. My friend, Sherae, who was sharing a Reiki session with me, felt the presence of a being and said, "There is a female here by the name of Billie and she wants you to know she is here now." It gave me great joy that Billie came to visit me during a healing session. It did not surprise me that she would find a way to appear from the other side.

Elderly people needed love and affection, but it never seemed that there were enough people to provide that. These patients, especially the ones with heart disease, could be a mystery because they could live a long time on hospice; therefore, the visiting staff became very fond of them.

I understood that I would eventually lose my patients, so I would put up walls to protect myself from the pain I knew was inevitable. But, I would still walk into the lion's den every workday because I knew I made a difference. I brought the light that they so desperately needed in their time of darkness. I never understood why I was given this gift, but I knew I would not walk away from it because I needed them as much as they needed me. This was much more than a job for me. It was my calling and I was grateful I listened.

My goal was to enjoy my life just like Billie told me to do. All I had was this present moment. If I was worried about the future, I could not be in the moment. If I was reliving the past, condemning myself for previous mistakes, I could not be in the moment. To hell with the economy and the fear-based politics; I did not need or want to go there. All I really had was this present moment right now.

I did not read the newspaper or watch the news on TV in five years and I recently stopped listening to the radio. As an empath, I would feel energy and I found that I absorbed the negative energy of mass media. What I witnessed were people's reactions to what was happening in the world. I decided to focus on love and to send love and healing to our planet instead.

It was hard to stay in a higher vibration when people all around were filled with fear. The belief in lack and limitation were contagious. But there was a reason for things to be collapsing and in chaos. They were dying in order to achieve a greater experience of life. The more we resisted it, the greater would be our pain. We had choice, always.

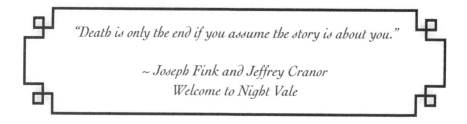

"Death is only the end if you assume the story is about you."

~ Joseph Fink and Jeffrey Cranor
Welcome to Night Vale

PART 2
My Journey

CHAPTER 14

Strawberry Music Festival

~ ❁ ~

9-5-2009

It was important for me to take time off from work for fun and relaxation because it was the balance that I needed. I was feeling sluggish and sleepy a lot and I did not need to see five patients a day. I wanted to walk in the park and cook more. I started arguing for my age limitation and figured that would not stop me. It was time to make a change.

I appreciated the generous paid time off that my hospice company provided. My husband, Gary, and I made a decision to travel to Central California, just south of Yosemite National Park, to attend the Strawberry Music Festival. We always loved this festival because of the diversity of the music that included folk, blues and country and it was wonderful at night when I could smoke and dance. I found joy in watching the children dance and sing. How fortunate they were to have parents who loved them and took them to this awesome festival!

Gary was so sweet to get up early and get good seats for us. I was so controlling by insisting that he brought water. He gave me a dirty look when it fell out of his pack for the third time and was reminded by some man in the crowd. I made amends by treating us to dessert and he was thrilled. It made my heart smile to bring him happiness. I knew I would get more joy out of life if I brought more joy to him.

I spent $100.00 that I had been holding onto for a long time. It felt good to buy a beautiful, flowing purple blouse and a cowboy hat with a strawberry appliqué. I was tempted not to buy these items for myself and it was a real breakthrough to face the fear and do it anyway. I have been thrifty all my life and found it difficult to spend money on myself. I needed to wear this cowboy hat often to remind me that there was an abundant universe that would provide. It was also another aspect of who I was: fun-loving!

I had an amazing conversation with a female photographer at the concert. She said she was able to be with her mom the last three months of her life. They talked about everything and her mom shared about the rape and abuse she endured as a child. This enabled the woman to have compassion for her mother's upbringing. When she told her brother about what her mother shared with her, he softened his perception of their mother. She had a peaceful death surrounded by her loving family.

Maybe I needed to let my kids know about my past. When I was 5-years-old, the ice cream man came to our neighborhood and I wanted to have it every day. My mom would tell me "No," but every Friday we would be able to have some. When Friday came and I wanted ice cream, she yelled at me for asking and I never felt worthy enough to have what I wanted since.

It would have been nice to return home on Monday so we would have an extra day at Yosemite, but Gary felt the need to work. Here I was, just outside of Yosemite, surrounded by the abundance of trees and beauty. Was this an area where I should push back my desires or go along with the program? Did I not get what I wanted because he was hard up for money? Maybe I needed to enrich my life on a daily basis with things that nourished my soul - like going to the beach, reading, yoga and 12-step program meetings.

I am so grateful that I found a 12-step program. I tried to control the people whose drinking bothered me to no avail. I had low self-esteem and troublesome relationships because I thought I had the answer for everyone. I have since learned to Live and Let Live. A 12-step program has enriched my life in ways I had never dreamed possible. Through this wonderful program, I learned to heal the wounds of my childhood while being surrounded by the love and support of my friends who loved me for who I am.

CHAPTER 15

Facing Fears

~ ❈ ~

10-26-2009

Yesterday, after talking with my friend Sherry, I made the decision to quit my full-time case manager job as a hospice nurse and switch to a per diem position with the same company. This was the most courageous thing I had done in my life. It would allow me to work when I wanted and on my own terms, but without the benefits. I was becoming so unhappy, drained and depleted. I could not get myself out of this rut, in spite of doing my best to be in gratitude.

I knew I had to face my greatest fear of not having enough. This fear was ruining my life and blocking the people to come to me for healing. I had to Let Go and Let God take care of me. I was holding on to that cliff for dear life and now that I was letting go, I was free to fly like the eagle on the vision board I created. I felt a huge weight had been lifted off my shoulders and I was giddy with relief. My friend, Julie, noticed that I looked many years younger and was glowing. Coincidentally, I did feel that way.

During my morning walk, I was listening to Ester Hicks' CD, *Abundance*, in which she would channel the higher consciousness of Abraham. It meant so much to me and I felt powerful. This was something that I needed to do every day to get through the next few weeks. I only had three weeks left to work full-time and I knew I did not want to come back after my November vacation. In my resignation letter, I stated that December 1st would be my last day as a full-time employee.

My telephone call to the executive director, Christine, was phenomenal. She was happy for me and said they all noticed a change in me. They could feel the disconnect I had from my job and saw how my face would light up when I talked about Reiki healing. I shifted my thoughts to a higher vibration whenever fear reared its ugly head and I would take deep breaths to allow and trust that the universe would provide for me always.

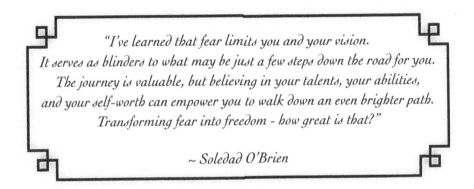

"I've learned that fear limits you and your vision.
It serves as blinders to what may be just a few steps down the road for you.
The journey is valuable, but believing in your talents, your abilities,
and your self-worth can empower you to walk down an even brighter path.
Transforming fear into freedom - how great is that?"

~ Soledad O'Brien

CHAPTER 16

8-4-2010

My Aunt Toni died yesterday and she was only 70-years-old. I was stunned. I remembered her smiling, joyful face the last time I saw her. She had a look of pride when she looked at me. Yesterday, I saw a chirping bird that was dancing in the bush a few feet away from a cat. I felt it was Aunt Toni's spirit telling me she was happy and that all was well. She was coming through from the other side to give her message of love and I felt at peace by feeling the joyfulness of her spirit. I asked Aunt Toni if she would help and guide me with writing this book. She gave me reassurance that she would be happy to do that.

I always believed that when we die, we drop all the pain, fear and anxiety that was accumulated over the years in order to transcend into the pure white light – the Light of Love – a bliss experienced beyond words.

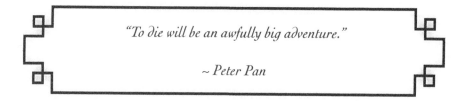

"To die will be an awfully big adventure."

~ Peter Pan

8-5-2010

My parents were still alive at 87 and 89-years-old. I knew the day was approaching for when I would lose my physical parents. It was painful to watch them age and to watch my mother's health decline. My greatest desire was to be with my mom when she crossed over because I would be able to take care of her physical and spiritual needs since I am a Reiki Master. During my last visit, I performed Reiki on her and she saw her guardian angel above her body. My mom was gifted and could see spirits and I was sure I acquired my gifts from her.

It was difficult for me to go back home to Chicago. I dealt with so much guilt about not being there for holidays, birthdays and other events. I hated Chicago winters and always loved California. My first husband wanted to expand our trucking business in California and I was happy to make that move. The energy of the beautiful Pacific Ocean was calling to my soul and I needed to be in a higher vibration as a healer.

Several months before, Mike, my youngest son who lived in Chicago, called me about this terrible abdominal pain he was experiencing. I told him to get to the hospital and worried about him for two hours. I heard from my ex brother-in-law that it was kidney stones and I was relieved that he had a problem that could be fixed. As a hospice nurse, I had seen too many young people die of cancer and those cases saddened me because I thought of the pain that I would feel if it were my own child.

I visited Chicago for Mike's wedding. He married a wonderful woman who was his childhood sweetheart when he was 15-years-old and Holly was 14-years-old. When Mike was in the 10th grade, we moved to California and they parted ways. Holly married someone else and had two girls. She was divorced when she saw Mike's Facebook post that he recently moved back to Chicago. They reconnected again and dated for one year before getting married. That beautiful wedding was a very special time for us. The band was playing my parents' favorite song. My mother left her walker next to the table and she and my dad waltzed on the dance floor bringing us all tears of joy!

47

During that visit, I told Mike that when it was time for me to make my transition, I intended to be happy and joyous. I hope he remembers my words as I will be ready for the next adventure. I want him to be happy for me to leave. I had seen too many families holding on to their loved ones because they did not want to face the inevitable loss. Families are too uncomfortable to talk about it and our culture turns its back on death. Many of us close our hearts to what is really important in life with things that go unsaid – like "I'm sorry" and "I love you." Our families can be a wonderful source of love and support. My hospice families have taught me so much about love, devotion and giving that comes from the heart.

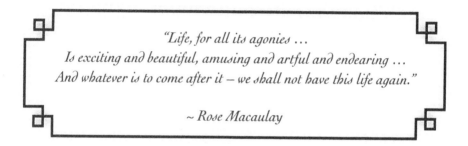

"Life, for all its agonies ...
Is exciting and beautiful, amusing and artful and endearing ...
And whatever is to come after it – we shall not have this life again."

~ Rose Macaulay

CHAPTER 17

My Shamanic Path

~ ❋ ~

8-7-2010

When I was attending an event, I ran into my old friend, Dana, whom I had not seen in years. She told me that Jamie, a shamanic healer who lived in Peru, would be coming to Laguna Beach to teach shamanic energy medicine. I felt a strong calling to follow up with this, so I asked Dana for Jamie's information.

Jamie had studied with the Four Winds, that was facilitated by Alberto Villoldo, PhD. I attended four classes with Jamie, which consisted of the four directions: north, south, east and west. I became a full mesa carrier and I learned how to do death rites through the Dying Consciously Program that assisted the soul to go straight to the light (www.dyingconsciously.org).

My close friend, Hanna, called to tell me about a good friend of hers on the East Coast who was caring for her dad that was on hospice. Her dad had not eaten or had anything to drink in the past week and had labored breathing and anxiety. All of his children were present and gave him permission to go to the light while reassuring him that they would take good care of their mom and that they would all be fine. They could not figure out why he was holding back from releasing his being and they were upset seeing him suffer in spite of the morphine.

Hanna asked me to do long-distance shamanic healing on this special man, who had been like a second father to her. I readily agreed and received a channeled message to do shamanic death rites on him while Hanna did long-distance Reiki. I was happy to oblige and I opened my mesa, a colorful wool cloth, that I purchased in Peru. Inside were my healing stones that were activated with shamanic energy during my training sessions with Jamie. I laid out my special Chopi beads, that were blessed by the shaman in Peru, to represent this man's chakras. I used a rattle over the beads to unwind the chakras counterclockwise in order for the soul to be released from the body. During the last section of the healing, I felt this beautiful man's soul release while giving that energy to the Earth Mother. I sent Reiki to him on his journey home to the divine.

Later that day, I sat down to have my lunch. Halfway through, I received a channeled message to call Hanna. She was happy to share her experience with this healing. She began doing Reiki and then was led to do theta healing on him. Theta healing alters the electrical rhythm of the brain with theta waves while altering one's consciousness. Hanna was able to energetically go to the light with the theta healing, so she symbolically held his hand and told him she would help him go to the light. He took her hand. Initially, she felt his fear and told him it was okay to let go. He was able to do so and they were both in a state of bliss as they traveled to the light. Hanna reached the top with him and told him she had to go back. Suddenly, the hand of his youngest daughter appeared who had died in a car accident at 20-years-old. His daughter took his hand and led him across the barrier with love and joy. I was thrilled to hear this because even though I have read stories like this in the past, it became very tangible to be a part of a miracle.

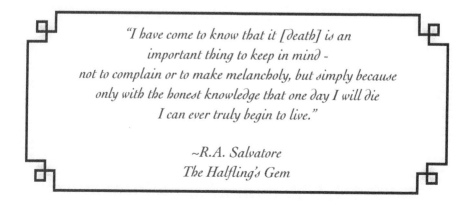

"I have come to know that it [death] is an
important thing to keep in mind -
not to complain or to make melancholy, but simply because
only with the honest knowledge that one day I will die
I can ever truly begin to live."

~R.A. Salvatore
The Halfling's Gem

8-12-2010

I was reflecting on the patients I had lost in the past years. As I thought of them, I knew they were paying me a visit and were enjoying the growth they had seen in me over the years.

8-18-2010

Yesterday, Margie's dad made his transition. He had been dealing with prostate cancer for a few years and was doing fairly well until it traveled to his bones. We talked about hospice for her dad on-and-off the past two years, but she would always say, "We're not ready for that yet." The decision was finally made because he was declining rapidly and they needed the support that hospice provided.

Margie wanted me to be their nurse, but since I made the wise choice to work per diem, I explained that I could only supplement the regular case manager who would be assigned to her father's case. I was delighted to be able to see him every other week. A week prior, he was sitting up, joking and laughing with us. I thought he would be with us for a while longer. Two days later, he took a turn for the worse.

I told Margie the story about doing death rites on my friend's surrogate dad. I told her I would be happy to do that for her dad when she felt the time was right. I explained I could do it energetically from a distance or in-person. She called and said she would like to do that and I decided to do it in-person. I was shocked when I saw her father's great decline.

He was now in a hospital bed, breathing irregularly, with the death rattle that was so common at the end of life. I opened a sacred space and was led to begin Reiki on him. I sensed his body beginning to relax and his breathing became less labored. I began the death rites that would unwind the chakras and clear them as I gave the negative energy to the Earth Mother to be healed. I coaxed his energy field – starting from the soles of his feet and I used my hands to bring the energy up toward his head. I felt a resistance at his first chakra which holds our connection to the earth plane and our tribe. I felt it again at the second chakra which holds our emotions and sexual energy. I communicated to him that it was time to go to the light; time to let go of fear. I assured him that his wife was waiting for him across the veil and everyone would be fine. I felt his resistance leave as I moved my hands further toward his head and then past his head to the heavens above. I released my breath to help him. I closed all his chakras with Florida water. He was still alive when I left, but I told Margie he would most likely make his transition within 24 hours.

The next morning, I was looking forward to going to my usual 8:00 a.m. yoga class. I had a momentary inclination to call Margie to see how her dad was doing, but another thought took its place as I looked for my yoga mat. After class, some girls asked me to join them for coffee. I was torn but decided to go.

When I arrived home, my husband was at the door with a concerned look on his face. I asked if there were any calls since I had left my cell phone at home. He replied that Margie called shortly after I walked out the door to inform me that her dad had passed at 1:35 a.m. Immediately, I felt guilt about not making the call earlier and for going to yoga and coffee.

A few minutes later, Margie called. I told her I had just arrived home and offered my condolences. She had not called hospice at that time. She waited because she wanted me there for the death pronouncement. When I arrived, the family was fairly composed, but I saw from her red eyes that there were lots of tears as she bade farewell to her dad. He had stopped breathing right after Margie had administered the last dose of morphine.

I had told Margie about my thought to call her, but my mind had scattered elsewhere. The family was fine about how it turned out and no one questioned the delay in calling the mortuary. Margie graciously accepted my apology and said, "It was all perfect." This was a lesson for me that I did not have to be perfect and that there was divine timing in all things.

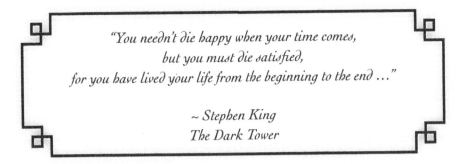

"You needn't die happy when your time comes,
but you must die satisfied,
for you have lived your life from the beginning to the end ..."

~ Stephen King
The Dark Tower

I felt blessed that I found this shamanic path to help others because a woman from the 12-step program called and asked if I could help her. She had a horrible childhood and was subjected to satanic rituals and abused until the age of 19 when she left the cult. She had Dissociated Identity Disorder and had 54 personalities; she was now down to 17.

She was advised to find a shaman and she thought of me. I told her that I would be happy to do shamanic healing on her. Her car broke down on the day she was to come for a treatment, so we rescheduled because I had some reservations about bringing her to my home. Regrettably, she ended up in a mental hospital and was released four days later when she called me again. The channeled message I received was to do energy work long distance, therefore, I used my special healing Chompi beads.

This distant healing was done while she was sleeping. I began with my pendulum over the chakras to determine how blocked they were. My pendulum indicated that all her chakras were closed. After doing the distant healing work, I tested again and the pendulum went in a circular motion which specified that they were all open. I had done about four healings on her that appeared to be very helpful.

The next day, she said she woke up much lighter and felt that something had been released. She was puzzled about the joyfulness of the other personalities – until she listened to my phone message that I had done a healing for her. She stated that all the other personalities were joyful and playing with the puppy she had lost six years ago.

All of a sudden, a thought occurred to me. I wanted to take her to the animal shelter and buy her a dog. This was so out of my character to spend $120 on an acquaintance, but I chose to do it anyway and walked through my fear. It was a magical and beautiful day that put pure happiness on her face when she held the little four-pound Chihuahua mix in her arms. I felt that this abandoned animal would be instrumental in her healing and it would reside in a good home with love. I was filled with joy that I made that possible. I was very blessed with good mental and physical health as well as a meaningful career that paid well in order to be of service to others – and for that, I was grateful.

CHAPTER 18

Taking Care of Myself

~ ❖ ~

I was listening to a psychologist on the radio who was talking about the "shadow side." She declared, "You see yourself as compassionate, but also have the shadow side of apathy." I saw myself in that statement because it was not easy to see the love and peace I brought to all of my patients and their families. It seemed that I was always left with the feeling that I had not done enough. I had witnessed so much pain and suffering that I felt I had to put walls up to protect myself. Unfortunately, the walls also prevented the love to come through, except for the few holes that were reserved for my sons, spouse, cats, and family members that I occasionally let in.

The walls were also the defense mechanisms that I developed during the difficult years of my childhood. I did not feel loved and accepted by my parents. I felt I needed to be the perfect daughter to get the love I desperately wanted. I was the proverbial people pleaser who wanted to make everybody happy except myself. As the eldest of five children, I readily stepped into the role of the "second mother" – especially to my sister, Angela, who was born when I was 10-years-old.

I excelled in school and I was criticized the first time I brought home a "C" on my report card. I lost my allowance for a month as punishment and shrugged it off as I had done with so many things. I felt undeserving and would not even treat myself because it was drilled into my head to save, save, save. Fortunately, I looked at my life as a beautiful unfolding process and I could spend money on myself when it felt right. I was learning to love myself.

My decision to step down from the stressful, full-time, Nurse Case Manager position was the best thing I had ever done for myself. I had the benefits of being my own boss and worked when I wanted to. I had the freedom to explore other interests such as building a healing practice, bike riding, and spending time at my beloved ocean where much needed healing occurred. I felt blessed to have this time and I was grateful for the benefits of being frugal because I had a lovely nest egg to dip into when needed. I was free. During this Letting Go process, I often heard the words from a Janis Joplin song: "Freedom's just another word for nothing left to lose."

I made the decision to take the whole month of September off and I looked forward to that. It was over 30 years ago since I had that much time off and it felt wonderful that I had allowed myself this precious gift.

8-23-2010

I was sitting at my favorite place in the world, Crystal Cove. I just loved being at this beautiful beach that was located 40 minutes south of my home towards Laguna Beach. I marveled at the divinity all around me, the magnificence of the ocean and the warmth I felt on my shoulders. I always loved the sound of the waves crashing over the rocks with little children laughing and playing.

While I was enjoying the beach, Aunt Toni came to visit me again from the other side. She was so happy and told me that she was here to help me write this book. Thanks, Aunt Toni!

I was sitting in a place of love because I had given myself the gift of per diem work that allowed me to have my own schedule and to live my life the way I wanted. Sadly, my job was stressing me out and my heart was not in it anymore. Letting go of my full-time job was so huge because it represented my "security," which included great benefits such as six weeks of personal time off, health insurance and a 401K.

When I started hospice, we had to write a one-page written note after each patient visit. Soon afterward, that became a two-page visit note that quickly grew to three pages. By September 2010, the visitation notes became four pages because the government was scrutinizing every little thing we would do as a result of their fear-based consciousness. When would all this craziness stop? When would we stop and ask ourselves, "What is the most important thing right now?" Certainly, it was being there for the patients and their families. Everyone said that, but it was the people who put their feet in the door to that hospice patient who truly understood what was important.

"If you celebrate your differentness, the world will, too.
It believes exactly what you tell it — through the words you use
to describe yourself, the actions you take to care for yourself,
and the choices you make to express yourself.
Tell the world you are one-of-a-kind creation
who came here to experience wonder and spread joy.
Expect to be accommodated."

~ Victoria Moran
Lit from Within: Tending Your Soul for Lifelong Beauty

CHAPTER 19

The past three years were very different for hospice care. Medicare was looking over our shoulder at everything that was written and that instilled fear for the people at the top. Hospice was living in fear that documentation was not good enough to cut the mustard and that Medicare would yank the money it forked over. What did they do with that fear? The stress would filter down to the nurses and they brought that negative energy to the patients.

What kind of world would we live in if we could just let go of fear? If we could all get connected into Universal Life Energy, God, Spirit, or whatever name you wanted to call it? It felt like the world was insane and it was trying to take us along in its fear-based consciousness.

I was at the beach and heard a father calling to his child. "Be careful. Look out for the algae; it is slippery." It was a good thing he didn't say, "Or you will fall," because the Universe would say "Yes" to what was said. Someone could choose who they were by their thoughts and actions because many of us were raised by fear-filled parents and they learned it from their parents and the cycle continued. What would my life be like if I would just let go?

One of the ways I learned to Let Go was to face my fear that my hospice company would disapprove of me if they knew I was doing Reiki treatments on their patients. When I first learned Reiki, I was very enthusiastic about using it and my hospice patients were the perfect recipients. I always asked the families if it was okay to give Reiki to their loved ones. Most were in agreement, because at that point, what would be the harm? I explained that I was a channel for God's healing energy and I consistently saw my patient's pain lessen and their anxiety diminish. All of the families were grateful for the treatments.

I attended a spiritual workshop in 2008 about following your dreams and made an agreement that I would follow my own dream about becoming a Reiki Master. I agreed to go on the Sedona Reiki website, register for the Reiki Master class and pay the $295 deposit. I faced fear, doubt and procrastination about my worthiness to proceed with my dream and I knew I had to have integrity to achieve it. I finished the sign-up process, and at the 19th hour, my life opened up.

I had to face my fear about taking an eight-hour drive alone to Sedona, Arizona. I chose to be responsible and see if my five-year-old Toyota was trip worthy. It was not and my car was ready for the road after spending $1,800 for major preventative work. I needed to spend money on gas as well as a bed and breakfast for lodging. I arrived in Sedona, without incident, and knew I had made the right decision.

The class was a full day on Saturday and Sunday and it was in a beautiful setting amid the majestic red rocks of this spiritual center. During the class, we had the opportunity to work on each other and I learned that my throat chakra was blocked; indicating that I was not speaking my truth. I knew immediately that it had to do with the "secret" Reiki treatments I was doing for my patients.

I had been doing Reiki on hospice patients since 2006. The very first time I utilized Reiki, I performed it on a patient who had insomnia and anxiety. She was able to sleep through the night and was more peaceful. I did not tell anyone at hospice about the healing work I was doing on patients. I decided that when I returned back to work, I would speak my truth about giving patients Reiki during my visits.

The following Tuesday, we had our hospice group meeting which included the doctor, managers and my peers. I took a deep breath; asked God for guidance; and announced, "I just returned from an amazing weekend in Sedona and I became a Reiki master. I have been giving Reiki treatments to my patients for the past three years with amazing results of decreased pain and anxiety." There was a moment of silence and the manager said, "Is that some kind of painting?" I explained it was energy work; adding that Reiki was used in hospitals to add some credence to the healing art.

Once I "came out of the closet", I felt freedom to share my experience with my peers and managers. I offered free energy sessions to everyone. At that time, only one woman accepted even though others talked about coming to see me for a treatment.

Our sweet volunteer coordinator was very excited and took up my suggestion to conduct a free in-service workshop about Reiki and energy healing. One of our hospice volunteers took Reiki I and II classes from me when I started teaching and continued to bless all the patients' lives she had touched.

I felt such a relief from being honest and it was time to be honest with myself. My struggle was about how much time I wanted to spend with hospice as opposed to doing healing exchanges with friends and spending time on the beach. I had a sense that I was going through a deep healing on all levels that was facilitated by the salt of the ocean, meditation and shamanic energy medicine. I continued to face my fears and not run away from them.

Another fear I faced was regarding health insurance. Medicare B was a lot of fear-based nonsense and I did not want any part of it. I decided to keep Medicare Part A because that would cover me if I was in the hospital as well as for hospice. If I broke a leg, I would be taken care of and if I was at the end of my life, I definitely wanted hospice.

I did not want all that fear-based stuff of Western Medicine. I did not want to go in for a blood pressure check just to have someone say I had high blood pressure and put me on medication. That would lead to another medication and another medication and that screamed total insanity to me.

I also did not want my breasts pressed to check for cancer. Two of my sisters had breast cancer. I chose not to entertain that thought because when it was my time to transition, then I would accept that and call upon hospice. It would be about facing death and surrendering to the will of God. I have made it this far and that was one reason I chose to let go of the fear of money.

Without health insurance, I would not know what was going on in my body. I believed it was not a bad way to live – to be happy and free. The other day, I heard about a gentleman who had a piece of plaque in his artery and he knew nothing about it. The plaque broke free and gave him an instant heart attack. This gentleman never had a medical problem; however, it was okay. It was his time to cross over and he would remain in spirit because we do not go anywhere when we die; we simply drop the shell of the body. There will be no greater Letting Go than death.

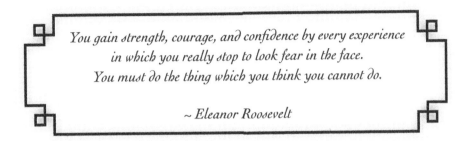

You gain strength, courage, and confidence by every experience in which you really stop to look fear in the face.
You must do the thing which you think you cannot do.

~ Eleanor Roosevelt

CHAPTER 20

Past Lives

~ ❄ ~

9-15-2010

I sat at Mile Square Park after an incredible healing exchange with my special friend, Kris, a Reiki Master. She gave me Reiki with massage and I gave her Reiki with shamanic healing. We both felt that we were getting the better end of the deal and we have done these exchanges for the past year.

Kris was blessed with the ability to tap into ancestry and the remembrance of past lives. She had an amazing channeling today, remembering a past life that she and I shared together as indigenous brothers. Kris was Sitting Bear and I was Running Elk.

In that lifetime, I had the ability to track by finding food and water. I was boldly confronted and eaten by a bear, so I lived a short life. I agreed to let this happen because my essence was part "bear energy" that brought about healing in a powerful way. I became the spirit guide for Sitting Bear who understood that this plan was in divine right order.

During my massage, Kris gently pulled my arm up and out. She told me to connect with Condor and I felt the connection in a huge way. When I turned over on my back, Kris massaged the front of me while Condor stayed above me and Bear remained sitting at my feet. When Kris and I hugged at the end of the session, we were deeply moved with tears as we gave gratitude for our beloved reunion.

The best time to release what no longer served us was during a full moon. Kris and I planned to do a full moon fire ceremony in two weeks. We envisioned our ceremony to be held in my backyard with the ancestors present who gathered in preparation. To call in the higher beings, a "Clearing Ceremony" was done first. We wrote on paper the things that we wanted released and threw it into the fire. I was looking for a partner to support me with a fire ceremony and my prayers were answered through Kris. Thank you, Spirit.

Kris shared that we came together in this lifetime as females in order to heal on a larger scale and complete the work of our destiny. It was about letting go and trusting in the divine plan – knowing that it was not an accident that our paths had crossed in our 60s.

I had always remained open to the possibility of past lives since I believed that life was eternal. I even had past life regressions through hypnotherapy and my shamanic classes which affirmed my belief.

*"Reincarnation isn't something in which
I choose to believe but rather a truth I accept.
Most people will never know the meaning of
their friendships, passions, choices and even challenges.
I embrace them, knowing that there's always
a perfect correlation between everything,
including between us and the ones
that love us and betray us at the end.
That's how I know I'm almost
never traveling somewhere but returning,
or not meeting someone but fixing the past,
or facing a challenge but ending a karmic cycle.*

*If I was a Buddhist Monk, a Scottish Doctor,
a French Monarch, or a Spanish Templar,
none of that really matters,
not as much as what I experienced
and believed during that time,
not as much as what I did ten years ago
or what I believed during my childhood,
not as much as who I am now and
what I can do with my life at present time."*

*~ Robin
Sacredfire*

CHAPTER 21

Hospice Per Diem

~ ❋ ~

9-23-2010

I sat on the beach and felt grateful that I had the gift of being able to do hospice per diem. A few days ago, hospice called and said that there was an important meeting for the nurses regarding the new paperwork. They invited me to attend the meeting and I thought, "Why not?" It would be paid for and it would be great to see some co-workers again. When I entered the room, I felt bad for the nurses that I saw. They looked so stressed due to the lack of staff and the high acuity of these patients. A rush of gratitude waved over me that I was no longer a monkey in that circus.

I walked away from that meeting with deep thoughts about fear-based consciousness. If people really knew who they were and where they came from, they would not be clinging to life at all costs. They would know that the ultimate of letting go was falling into the loving arms of God, or to the light, or to heaven.

What I knew for sure was that we were eternal beings having the choice to incarnate again or be on another level of consciousness that was better than the one before. The world would be a better place if everybody would shut off their TVs, computers and phones and go outside to connect with others.

My deepest thought came to me … "Love is being of service to another. Love is all there is." I felt like I was a channel for these words to come forth. I needed to know that I was a blessing to the world and to myself. I knew that we were all connected, so what was done for others should also be done for ourselves. When I gave out love, that was what came back to me. I believed that we were always expanding and getting better.

Last Sunday when I was on-call, the manager requested that I visit a patient who was transitioning. I was upset because I was with my husband at a festival and did not want to leave. When I arrived, I remembered the patient from when I made a visit a couple of months ago.

The family members had a lot of questions that I answered and I also reinforced the anti anxiety instructions of morphine and Ativan. I was receiving intuitive messages that told me to do Reiki on him and I shared this with the family. I asked if they would allow me to give him a Reiki treatment and they agreed.

After I finished Reiki on my patient, I sensed that his breathing slowed down and his anxiety lessened. One family member asked how long he had to live. I confided that I could not accurately predict the end of life, however, I felt he had a week since he was eating and drinking that day. One of the girls said she wanted to be there when he took his last breath and I explained that the soul decided when it was ready to depart. Being surrounded by their loved ones wanting them to stay would retain the person on the earth plane, even though the soul would be drawn to go to the light.

I was surprised when I found out the next day that my patient died. I gathered enough courage and called the son to share my condolences. I told him I was sorry that I thought his dad had longer to live and felt awful that I told the family he had a week since they wanted to be there for his passing. He reassured me that it was perfect the way it happened because he did not want to see his father going through more bad days of respiratory distress, anxiety and pain. He also shared that he felt the Reiki helped his dad to become more peaceful and relaxed and it gave him a spiritual release so that he would let go and go to the light.

It truly is all love on the other side of the veil. Love is the only thing that is real; all the rest is a game we are creating together. We choose the roles to take on for the evolution of our souls and it is the contrast of going through pain that we find joy. Our pain teaches us our greatest lessons. This is especially true with painful relationships.

Every person was in our lives for a reason – to give us the opportunity to learn something important about ourselves. Each person we encountered would provide such unique, valuable lessons that we needed to learn. I learned that I cannot predict how long someone had to live. If a family member was meant to cross over, then it would happen.

I was so grateful for my decision to change to per diem status with hospice because it allowed me to go on an amazing trip to Peru. This adventure changed my life and I was accompanied by my shaman friend, Isabella. When Isabella told me about it, my soul was shouting "Yes" to the opportunity of traveling to a foreign land. There were four of us – two males and two females – and we all became close friends from the experiences we shared. It was a special time for deeply anchoring in the divine feminine and the divine masculine and the healing that took place on that trip was priceless.

We traveled by train to Machu Picchu and I marveled at the changing scenery as we drew closer to our destination. I was so indebted that I was able to experience the wonder and magic of Peru with its ancient history and beautiful people. The energy of that magical land will remain forever in my memory.

CHAPTER 22

Mom's Decline

~ ❊ ~

9-25-2010

I made the airline reservations to fly back to Chicago so that I would be there for my mother's 88th birthday on October 26th. Mom was declining and was back in the hospital again. This had happened so many times this year. The doctors had administered numerous tests and everything returned negative, so this told me that it was psychosomatic. There was a part of me that became annoyed with my mom and that she was doing this for attention. She was a very frightened woman and was criticized as a child. I knew this because I was highly critical of myself and also criticized as a child.

I realized that I had built a protective wall around me so I would not feel the pain of suffering and death. That was why I had lasted so long as a hospice nurse. However, the wall had prevented love from flowing in and I felt like this little girl who was afraid her mommy would leave her.

My sister, Roxanne, sent me a text message that said Mom was in the hospital again because she was so fatigued and not able to get out of bed. I thought it was another one of her shortness of breath episodes, but it turned out her heart was not working effectively. Roxanne said she looked terrible and had lost a lot of weight. Roxanne finally agreed it was time for hospice because Mom said she would rather die at home.

I did not want to think about my mother dying as I felt this deep pain in my heart when I thought about losing her. I would not be able to hear her voice when I called and it was hard to imagine my mom not being there anymore. I needed to focus on the many telephone calls, the good times we had together, the quality of time spent and the bond of love that we shared instead of the guilt about all the things I had not done. I knew it was time to step up to the plate because if I was meant to be there at the time of her transition, then I would be there. I had confided in my mom that I wanted to be with her during her final weeks and knew she was relieved to hear that.

I wanted to take this journal with me to Chicago and read it to my mom because I felt it was time to heal this pain once and for all. I wanted to ask my mother to be in touch with me after her transition and to channel me what it was like on the other side. I wanted the opportunity to share this with the world so others would not need to be in fear.

CHAPTER 23

My Nursing History

~ ❁ ~

I always had a hard time making decisions, however, I found that the right answers were there when I sought from within. Even though I had made mistakes in the past, that did not mean that I could not trust myself to make important decisions in my life journey. I learned to trust my inner wisdom.

I remembered watching the soap opera, *All My Children*, and one of the characters was a nurse. I identified with that very strongly and it was like a thunderbolt hit me – the realization that I knew my life path. I went back to school in 1977 when my sons were four and six. I went to school part-time as I wanted to be there for my children. It took four years to complete my Associate's Degree in Nursing at Moraine Community College.

My first job was in the operating room because it was primarily weekdays with weekends on-call. Eventually, I was fired because I had a difficult time with the sterile procedures that were required and I did not want to hide behind a surgical mask. I needed to have a closer connection to the patients, so God did for me what I could not do for myself.

I went to a different hospital to try another job in the operating room. I was on the verge of being fired again when I asked a co-worker what her favorite area of nursing was. She told me she liked being a Hemodialysis Nurse because one of the benefits was having Sundays and holidays off. My inner guidance told me to explore this field.

I was grateful to be free of the hospital setting and found a job about three miles from my home. I held that RN position for four-and-a-half years and enjoyed the connections I made with the patients that came in for treatment three times a week. But ultimately, I was ready for a change.

I decided to give home health nursing a try as I was enticed by the freedom and autonomy that it afforded. I started on a part-time basis while living in Chicago until my ex-husband and I moved to Southern California in 1989.

Upon settling into our new home in California, I began working for a company that administered IVs in the home setting. At that time, AIDS was rampant and it was in my job description to administer IV meds and nutrition to those unfortunate people. I became very vigilant with the used needles while carefully placing them in the containers and thoroughly washing my hands. I saw the pain in those patients' eyes and I could do nothing about it except to call the doctor who would prescribe pain meds that were inferior to morphine. That was not where I was meant to be.

In 1991, I started working for Quality Continuum Home Health. The part-time position turned into full-time and I absolutely loved the connections I made with patients as their Case Manager. Finally, I was in love with my job!

There seemed to be a trend at our home health company to take care of terminal patients under the home health umbrella. For the most part, doctors would shy away from the conversations regarding end-of-life issues. They left that for the social workers in the hospitals because that was where our referrals came from.

I found myself getting many terminal patients who wanted to remain at home. Families took time off work and flew in from neighboring states to help with the caregiving needs of their terminal loved ones. As they faced the reality of losing someone they loved, I was humbled to assist them with their emotions as well as unresolved issues and conflicts that would arise

Instinctively, I knew I was good at what I was doing, but I was unsure whether I could face death and dying every day. I prayed about it; asked God to give me a sign; and it was not long before an opening became available in the hospice division of the company I worked for.

I applied, but another RN filled the position. Luckily, I was elated that I did not get that RN position because I learned that it was visiting patients in nursing homes – which I thoroughly detested! I just wanted to share my experience, strength and love in the comfort of a patient's home with their loved ones surrounding them. That was what I was searching for in hospice.

In those days, it was common for people to not have an understanding of what hospice was all about. Hospice was for patients who had a diagnosis of six months or less. Many patients died within a week or two when they could have benefited from hospice service months before. If only their doctor had the courage to have those honest end-of-life discussions because it was clear that the amount of fear surrounding death was palpable. Many families told me they wished they had hospice much earlier than they did.

A few days later, I saw my friend, Dawn, and told her I was still interested in hospice. She mentioned that she just heard about an RN position that entailed visiting patients in their home. She instructed me to talk to the nursing supervisor, Darcy. I went and saw Darcy who knew me from our home health division. She was excited about my enthusiasm and the passion I had for working with terminal home health patients. The next day, I was told that the position was mine! I was ecstatic and scared at the same time, however, I knew that my path was divinely guided and I was where I was supposed to be.

My decision to become a nurse was one of the best decisions I made. What a journey it has been to look back on how it all started and where I am today.

CHAPTER 24

The Joys of Per Diem Hospice

~ ❃ ~

9-30-2010

Another meeting at hospice, spending two-and-a-half-hours going over more paperwork – which had now increased to a four-page report! I could not believe they were paying me for the time I was spending in this oppressive office. I knew I had to be productive since working only two days a week gave me the structure I needed, an income and the sweet joy of five days off.

One of the advantages of per diem hospice was that I was able to see my two long-term patients every other Wednesday. One was a fairly strange relationship and the other was a real sweetheart that I really looked forward to spending time with. I felt a real connection to Carolyn in a rather strong way. The tension was sometimes high in her home, especially if there was drama going on with her husband or the kids. She and her daughter were enmeshed with each other and neither of them had been able to cut the umbilical cord.

When I was in Peru and did my plant medicine, I had a vision that I put my arms around Carolyn. We were heading past the veil, where the separation from human life into heavenly beings was, and then transcended into the oneness. We were both filled with joy as we ascended, but when we got to the top, Carolyn chickened out and went back to earth. I had broken through the veil to experience great love and bliss as well as the feeling of being connected to everything – the oneness. I told her about it and mentioned it again to be sure, but maybe I was afraid of being judged.

CHAPTER 25

Letting Go and Letting God

10-2-2010

I felt so thankful to live in Southern California, but I felt guilty that I was not in Chicago as my mom went through this medical nightmare. I was sitting at the beach with the sun on my face while looking at the ocean. I could not leave this sweet spot because I had done so much healing by connecting to Pachamama – an Incan mythological goddess of the Andes representing Mother Earth. I was told that I was chosen to heal the wounds of the ancestors that the shamanic path had called to me. I wanted to heal my mother's wounds as well – not the physical ones, but the spiritual ones – and I decided that I would do a shamanic treatment every day that I was with her.

I was informed that Mom was transferred to the nursing home. I called her to let her know that we were dealing with this as best we could. I told her that I would be there when they decided to discharge her. I shared this book with her and said that my purpose in writing it was to help people understand that there was no death; there was only eternal life and to be where God was.

I knew I had to heal the wounds of the past and I began that by stepping into my role as a shaman. I chose to pray and be the light for the whole family because I needed to keep my vibration up. I had a plan to be with my mom for the majority of her day. I was trying to control this thing that cannot be controlled – my life. As I was told in my spiritual program, I needed to Let Go and Let God. Letting go for me has been my journey and I needed to trust that God was in charge.

My way of dealing with life is through journaling because it is so cathartic. My true feelings come out when I sit with pen and paper. It was helpful to look back in my journal to see how far I had come and it was also interesting to see how things had a way of working out. I recommend it to anyone. The best way to get started is to sit down first thing every morning and write for five minutes.

10-9-2010

It was difficult to think about losing my mom. What would life be like without her? Would I still feel her presence? She told me she felt my presence all the time. Somehow, she was connected to my healing powers. Please, Mom, stay alive until I was able to visit.

This was a tough day in so many ways. I called Mom at the nursing home and her TV was blaring. I asked her six times to shut it off and she did not comprehend what I said. She never was a good listener and now it was even worse. She asked appropriate questions about my family, but the lights went out when I responded.

My visit for Chicago was in 12 days and I did not know what to expect. I was sure I would experience shock as my sisters said mom's progress was at a snail's pace and I felt they were right. I wanted her to be out of the nursing home by the time I arrived so I could take care of her.

I firmly believed it was time for hospice. I was anticipating that certain family members would be resistant to the idea. I needed to keep my vibration level high because my whole family would need to be uplifted. I knew from my years of experience as a hospice nurse that the worst comes out in people when they must face the death of a loved one ... especially a parent.

We all had choices and could just as easily choose peacefulness and love. It was about surrender and acceptance when it boiled down to everything in life, particularly when facing the illusion of death. I had seen so much suffering in my years of nursing and wondered why some very sweet souls were taken at such young ages. Recently, I had two patients who died young: the 21-year-old man and the 32-year-old woman with cancer. It was utterly devastating to their families when a loved one died so young. I could not even go there.

Last Monday was my 10th wedding anniversary and I called my mom. She sounded so weak and frail that I spent an hour crying after I ended the call. I had tried to be so strong, but I put up another shield to protect me – like I had done all my life. I just wanted to run away from the pain of losing my mom.

I needed to face this fear about confronting others as I do not stand up for myself. If others had an opinion about something, I assumed they were right and I was wrong. This lesson was coming to me often, so I knew I needed to resolve it.

I went to the hospice office to turn in paperwork and saw one of my co-workers. She said our executive director, Christine, was fired and escorted out of the office. I felt sad because Christine was a kind person who was well-liked. There was so much tension in the air that it could have been cut with a knife because they had an interim executive director who was a real monster. The environment was toxic because the message to all of us was, "You are not good enough. You can do better!" Unfortunately, that was the universal consciousness and it was magnified in the microcosm of Corporate America.

I heard it often that when people were so stressed, it affected their family life. Dad came home tense and took it out on Junior, unless Dad stopped at the bar beforehand and came home in a rage. Then he took it out on whoever was in his way, permanently scarring the little ones who absorbed the pain and felt it was their fault that there was so much sadness in their home.

I heard that when a fish dies, it dies from the head down and that was what was happening to Corporate America as well as my hospice company. I saw a definite shift when our hospice became a publicly traded company. It was all about the numbers and the push to get admissions. I saw the look of tension in the nurses' faces when I attended the Thursday meetings and I knew they were all overloaded with work due to being short two nurses. I was so grateful that I made the decision to Let Go and Let God regarding my per diem position when I became my own boss.

CHAPTER 26

Dorothy

—❋—

10-11-2010

I was riding my bike at the beach with my new friend. My cell phone rang while we were enjoying our conversation while sipping on some orange juice and taking in the ocean air. I rarely answered my phone when I was with others and let the calls go to voicemail. I knew it was hospice and I decided not to listen to the message until I rode back to my car about 45 minutes later. I assumed that they did not have a Registered Nurse to do an intravenous visit.

When I listened to the message, it was about Dorothy. She was one of the long-timers and one of my favorite patients that I could not bear to let go. The message said that Dorothy was actively dying. Since I was her Case Manager for the past four years, hospice thought they would give me the opportunity to make the visit since I was very close to the family.

I asked my pendulum if I should work today and it said, "No." My pendulum is an elongated, pointed crystal that is wrapped in copper wire that hangs on a long chain around my neck. I pray over it first and ask the higher beings to be with me as I ask a question. It spins in a circle for "Yes" and remains still for an answer of "No." I used it frequently when I needed answers.

I really wanted to see Dorothy. I was perplexed as to why my pendulum gave me a "No" answer although I wanted to run away and not face her death. I called her daughter, Sandy, who said Dorothy was a bit better and that calmed me. She said it would be best to visit her mother and I headed over to their house.

On my way to Dorothy's house, I received another call from the office asking if I could fit in another visit. I told them I would see how my afternoon was going. By the time I got to Dorothy's place 10 minutes later, I called them back and said I could not make another visit. The old me would have jumped at the chance to make extra money.

While I climbed the steps to the back door, I asked God and my spirit guides to give me the right words. When I saw Dorothy, I burst into tears. She was so weak and frail with her beautiful blue eyes glossed over. I kissed her and told her I loved her. She gave me her usual angelic smile and my whole being soared. Maybe she wanted to make her exit now before I saw my mom in 10 days.

Dorothy said several times during our two-hour visit, "I'm going home." When we were taking her back to bed from the bathroom, she pointed to "someone" who was standing in front of us. There was no one else in the room. "I can see the spirit guides and the angels," she said. "Do you see them standing there?" Neither of us saw anything.

Dorothy always liked the Reiki healing treatments that I had done for her when I made my visits. I had felt myself pulling away from her a bit these past several months. I believed on some level that I knew we would lose her soon, so I asked her if she would like me to do the shamanic work on her and she agreed. It felt good to show her my mesa, a healing tool that was a small cloth with stones. I explained that I would use my rattle to unwind the chakras and it would remove any negative energy. I doubted that she understood as she was not able to communicate her usual joy after she received Reiki. But, I knew it was there because I felt the love I had for her and it was flowing strongly through my hands. This would happen when I am one with God while channeling that beautiful healing energy.

It made me question why I blocked this energy sometimes. What was the fear behind it? The universe I was born into was an immense consciousness made of love, joy, acceptance and giving. The giving aspect had been a difficult area for me, although I received such radiant joy when I gave of myself.

10-19-2010

It had been over a week since my last visit to see how things were going with Dorothy. It was a roller coaster ride with good days and bad days. I was surprised she lived into this week, but this had happened before. She had her two daughters and daughter-in-law at her home and awakened after being surrounded by her loved ones. Her writing teacher came to visit with a bouquet of flowers and arrived shortly after I did. I gathered information about the past week's events and assembled the paperwork together.

At the end of my visit, I asked Dorothy if she wanted Reiki and she readily agreed. We both were sitting at the edge of the bed. I had my arms around her and I was getting ready to lay her down. I gave her the choice of how she wanted to receive Reiki and she preferred to stay like we were. I felt the love come through my hands and the beautiful energy came forth. My tears started falling as I held my precious patient in my arms for maybe the last time. I whispered in her ear that I loved her and I asked her to visit me from the other side and send me a message. She said she would and told me she loved me, too. I will never forget this precious one. I told her not to be afraid because she was going into love and it would be joyful and beautiful.

Knowing our time together was coming to an end, I climbed down the stairs with a heavy heart. I talked to her daughter and she told me that Dorothy said "someone" was around her wanting to take her somewhere, but she did not want to go. I shared with her daughter that most people felt fear when they were nearing the end of their lives. It was a tough thing to ultimately let go, but it was something we all have to do in the end. Dorothy was still talking about going home.

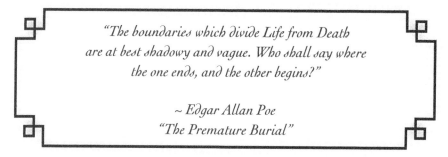

"The boundaries which divide Life from Death are at best shadowy and vague. Who shall say where the one ends, and the other begins?"

~ Edgar Allan Poe
"The Premature Burial"

CHAPTER 27

My Chicago Visit

~ ❋ ~

10-20-2010

Before leaving to Chicago tomorrow, I went to an awesome spiritual workshop at the Church of Religious Science in Huntington Beach. We were taught a technique to go to the light with worrisome thoughts. I volunteered and it worked beautifully for me. I was able to get in touch with my feelings instead of running away from them. It began by taking a deep breath while holding those feelings at my heart center. When I exhaled, I visualized taking the feelings and worries to the edge of the universe where the veil was. I was able to deposit my worries about my mom there. I felt a great burden lift from my heart and surrendered to God's will for my mother because I knew that this was her journey.

When I arrived in Chicago, my intent was to see my mom on Friday night. I wanted to stay with her the first night as I envisioned this to be a special time for my parents and me. I needed to put my anxieties and concerns aside for the welfare of my mom and dad because it would be beneficial for all of us.

I talked to my sister, Angela, who attended the discharge meeting at the nursing home for Mom. I told her to let them know that we would take Mom home Saturday morning and to arrange for the durable medical equipment such as a bedside commode, oxygen and a walker.

10-22-2010

I arrived in Chicago around 2:00 p.m. and went straight to the nursing home where my mother was residing. Mom had such a joyful look of surprise when I walked in the door and I gave her a big hug and kiss. Then, I proceeded with a foot massage while she listened to beautiful music on my iPod. Her skin was still good, but with so much muscle wasting away, she was down to 105 pounds. It was so difficult to see her decline and I had a hard time holding back my tears.

10-23-2010

Mom was discharged from the nursing home. It was good to have her back home, but she had a hard time getting out of the chair and transferring to the bed. I wondered if she would get any stronger.

10-24-2010

I awoke at 5:15 a.m. and was not able to get back to sleep. Dad and I just finished putting Mom back to bed after she fell trying to using her bedside commode. She looked so weak and helpless lying there on the floor. The next thing she said to me was, "I didn't think it would end like this." My heart sunk and broke for her. I could not fix this. I knew I was losing my mom. I felt so sad.

10-28-2010

It was Mom's 88th birthday on October 26th and I was still trying to assimilate what had transpired. My dear younger sister, Angela, stayed at Mom's with me for the past couple of nights and it was a godsend. That morning, she and I took a long walk with the dogs and discussed that Mom would need a caregiver when I left since none of us had the ability to do this job 24/7. We agreed that we needed to have a family meeting in the afternoon. We also talked about staying in the light and being the light for our family. Our mother's decline was having a toll on all of us.

I decided to do a shamanic and Reiki treatment for our sister, Roxanne, which mellowed her out. I had sent Reiki to the meeting and to my family. I continued to pray the whole time and asked for God to help us all. I held my arms upward to the light, and Donna De Lory's song, "Believe, Believe" kept coming into my head. I shared with my sisters about being in the light. Angela and I hugged Roxanne tight and told her we loved her. I reminded them that nothing can over take love. I asked them to breathe in the light and said, "Allow." It was all about Letting Go and Letting God. It was simple. God was omnipresent … a continual presence who was ever loving and ever caring for me and my loved ones.

My brother, Sam, arrived at my parent's home a short time later. He told us about a Lithuanian lady he knew who was out of a job and had many years of caregiving experience with letters of recommendations. Angela was delighted that Sam knew of someone and we set up a time for her to come over.

We sat around the small kitchen table and laughed about funny stories from the past. That really lightened the energy. We decided to eat the delicious dinner Angela prepared. Angela invited Sam to Thanksgiving dinner. Although it was a long way off, anything could happen.

After the dishes were cleared, the first caregiver arrived. Her heart was full of love. She spoke little English, although she understood what was said. She did not own a car, so my dad offered to drive her home at night.

The next interview was Nicole, Sam's friend. She was upbeat, efficient and loving. Mom and Dad both expressed their preference for her and hired her as the caregiver. It was difficult for them to spend money, but they realized it was a necessity. Both of my parents came from the Depression Era and suffered scarcity consciousness

10-31-2010

I arrived home and was feeling peaceful while sitting on the beach after my spiritual program meeting. Gary left yesterday to visit his daughter in Georgia, so I had the house to myself for five days.

I had some amazing conversations with Angela and she shared with me that she went to a party the day after Mom's birthday. She told me she met a couple at the party who could read people's energy. This couple told her that she had an amazing aura and that her energy and vibration was high. Angela attributed this to the healing that came with forgiveness for our brother.

I felt that I held the torch during my visit and handed the torch to Angela who would be instrumental in helping Roxanne come to the light of forgiveness and healing. Roxanne was on her path and I simply needed to honor the path that she had chosen. I expressed to her that Sam was her greatest teacher. She did not understand until I explained how my dear husband was my greatest teacher because he inspired me to look at my fears regarding lack and limitation consciousness.

I continued to send distant healing to my mom and she felt the energy. It was wonderful that she was spiritual and open to my talks about death. On the contrary, my dad felt that when you died, all that was left were the memories. I shared with both of them the stories of my patients who were close to death and saw their loved ones who had crossed over. This brought them comfort to realize that their loved ones were around them after leaving their bodies.

CHAPTER 28

Quitting Hospice

---❈---

11-21-2010

I attended a "Healing the Inner Child" workshop in Laguna Beach. I felt that part of my armor had been stripped away in that class. My intuition whispered to let go of the job and trust that something wonderful would take its place.

I called my dear friend, Sherry, and confided that I was very unhappy with my job and was seriously considering to quit. Her response back was, "How does that make your soul feel?" I exclaimed, "Free." I made the decision to quit my job.

I realized I was scheduled to see two patients this week, but my heart was not into it. I had been off for two weeks and just did not want to go back. The energy was terrible and I felt that I no longer belonged there.

I finally decided to call my manager. I gently told her I would be leaving hospice by stating, "Christine, I cannot do this anymore. I need to quit this job. I cannot watch another person die." She shared that she saw a change in me and she noticed that every time I spoke about Reiki, I would light up. She said she saw Reiki as my path and wished me well. I replied graciously, "I know myself. I may be tempted to collapse in fear and try to get my job back. Don't let me do it!" She responded back emphatically, "All right Mary, I won't!"

I decided that I would give it until next November to see if I missed hospice or needed the extra money. If I felt drawn to continue, then I would go somewhere else as my current company had lost its soul.

11-22-2010

I woke up and found the sun shining when I thought it would be raining. I saw this as a test to my resolve of releasing my job. Gary left for an appointment, so I would not have to explain where I was going. I asked God for a sign if I was not supposed to quit and nothing came. Even though I was feeling fearful, I knew I had to move forward and finally retire.

When I arrived at the hospice office, I unloaded one box of supplies and two boxes of forms and miscellaneous paperwork. I put my handwritten resignation letter on top. I walked into the manager's office while she was on the phone and put the envelope on her desk. I left the supplies in her room and I brought in the other two boxes for them to recycle. I said my farewells and shared about my miracle story of freedom to live the life I so desired and my co-workers were happy for me.

I went home and I told my husband. He was so happy for me, too, which was really cool. He said he knew how discontent I was and he was proud of me for having the courage to quit my job. It felt wonderful that I had his love and support.

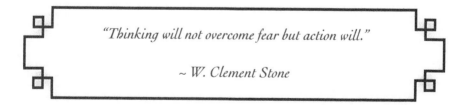

"Thinking will not overcome fear but action will."

~ W. Clement Stone

CHAPTER 29

Dorothy's Transition

~ ❈ ~

Dorothy was my favorite patient and was facing death soon. I had not seen her in two weeks due to my shamanic training, so the changes in her were very apparent and I was surprised she was still with us.

I had been blessed to see Dorothy every other week for a year. I made the decision to visit Dorothy, as a friend, without the restrictions of being a paid employee of a company and I saw her when I wanted. She was the one who kept me in hospice for so long. She was such a sweetheart with laughing, sky-blue eyes. Dorothy was also a gifted writer and was honored to share in this book.

It brought me pain to see her so frail and dying. I knew I was still running away and that I needed to face her death with my presence. I mentioned to Dorothy's eldest daughter, Duchess, that I wanted to be there when her mom made her transition so I could give her Reiki. Duchess thought it was a great idea and reflected on how much Dorothy loved Reiki.

11-25-2010

I received a text message from Dorothy's other daughter, Sandy, that said, "Mom is in a semi-coma, but is comfortable." I was stunned because I thought it was about my mom until I recognized Sandy's phone number. I said a prayer of thanks that I still had my mom and

I called Sandy to ask about Dorothy. She expressed that it was close and asked hospice to make a visit.

I felt torn because I had 14 people coming for Thanksgiving dinner and could not go to Dorothy. After all my guests departed, I called about 8:30 p.m. and Dorothy was about the same. I was too tired to make a visit, so I sent a prayer and distant Reiki.

11-26-2010

My intuition was nudging me to visit Dorothy, so I called her family to ask if the late afternoon would be okay. Sandy replied, "You are welcome here whenever you want to come." Upon arriving at her home, I found Dorothy a bit fidgety with her eyes half-opened. I kissed her and told her I loved her, adding that it was okay to go home to God and not to be afraid.

I checked Dorothy's vital signs but could not measure her blood pressure which was typical when a patient was near death. Her heart rate was increasing and her lungs were clear. I tested her chakras with my pendulum and found the lower four were blocked. The pendulum swung in a counterclockwise direction which indicated that Dorothy was out of balance. I proceeded with a 20-minute Reiki session as well as the shamanic death rites that integrated all the chakras and freed them to be released from the body when the soul decided to depart. After the treatment, I checked her chakras again with my pendulum and they were all spinning in a clockwise direction which told me she was balanced and happy.

When I left Dorothy after my last visit, I told her daughters to call me when she was making her transition and they agreed. I slept with my phone next to my bed and awoke the next day to Sandy's text message: "Mom is dancing in heaven at 12:15 a.m. Saturday." I felt the tears well up, but then received a very peaceful feeling that Dorothy was happy. She was free of a body that no longer functioned and she no longer needed continuous oxygen, a diaper, or a walker to take a few steps.

I called Sandy and she said that Dorothy was so peaceful when she took her last breath. Sandy and I had an amazing conversation about her journey with her mother and how it taught her what love was all about. She shared that her mom had a very difficult labor with her and had stated, "I don't think I can do this." Her sister told her, "This last child of yours will be a great comfort to you in your old age." That was exactly what happened. The care that Sandy gave her mom was kind, loving and a great gift.

I heard this so many times in my hospice years of how wonderful it was to care for a parent. I have always admired the dedication I observed and did not believe I was capable of such a challenge. I also have a new respect for caregivers since I spent a week caring for my mom. My mom was doing well as I was doing remote Reiki healing on her.

12-2-2010

Before Dorothy died, I asked her to give me a sign that she was okay after she crossed over. Dorothy loved scarves and during one of our visits, she gave me one of her scarfs as a gift.

I was in my healing room when a strange thing happened. As I was preparing to light my candle for my morning meditation, the scarf Dorothy had given me was on my altar. It started to move and knocked off the small bottles that were on the edge. I immediately thought it was our cat and looked down to scold him for playing with the scarf, but there was no cat there.

I thought of Dorothy and felt her presence and love. Her message to me was that life did exist on the other side and it was beautiful. I knew she was very proud of me for letting go of my job and taking the freedom I deserved.

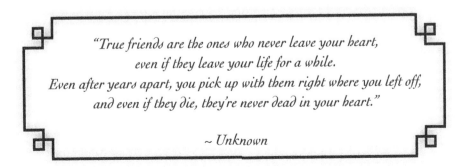

"True friends are the ones who never leave your heart,
even if they leave your life for a while.
Even after years apart, you pick up with them right where you left off,
and even if they die, they're never dead in your heart."

~ Unknown

CHAPTER 30

Christmas Eve

~ ❄ ~

12-24-2010

It was Christmas Eve and I sat at the beach in order to nourish myself in the energy of the beautiful ocean. My mom was back on antibiotics and her diarrhea returned with a vengeance. My sister planned to stop at the health food store to get some probiotics as I was preaching about it for the past several months. I did remote healing on Mom last night and in the morning. All her chakras were blocked except for the upper two. When I was done, they were all spinning open.

Having been through so many difficulties with my own family and my hospice families over the years, I was reflecting on the stressors that arose when a loved one was declining. Those stressors could put families at odds with one another. Part of being a hospice nurse was being an advocate for my patient and it often meant that I would have heart-to-heart conversations with family members.

How could I stay in a place of love? How could there be peace in the world if we could not find peace within ourselves? Why did I feel like I could fix everybody? Where do I go with all of this? I decided to ask God to intervene and let go of it all.

My life was so wonderful in California away from the craziness of my conflicted family. Everyone was on their own path and it was not for me to judge a person's direction. I would let things be and allow the process to unfold as it should. Maybe in a month, some kind of healing would occur. I had to ask myself, "What would love do?" I chose to be the love.

CHAPTER 31

Fears Around Money

~ ❄ ~

1-22-2011

I intended to be a clearer channel and I needed to start with my house and car. I came to the realization that my car represented me and I did not take care of my car or myself. I had a blind spot. I knew my car was dirty and I would apologize whenever anyone rode in it. I was cleaning out my life and it felt good. When I retired, many things happened because I decided to Let Go and Let God. It was the hardest thing I ever had to do. The more I faced my fears, the more I saw that miracles were happening!

I called my friend to detail my 2001 Toyota Camry. I struggled with spending $175 for detailing as well as $225 to do the clay bar which made the exterior shiny and new. I felt the familiar resistance about spending money, so I asked my pendulum and it affirmed to do both.

I had a great deal of fear about driving to Los Angeles and spending money on New Year's Eve, but I did it and it was incredible! Gary and I attended a yoga party with Donna De Lory singing her beautiful, spiritual music that we both loved. We danced and sang and brought the New Year in right!

I put down the deposit for our trip to Bali and we decided to extend it another five days. Abundance came from the consciousness that my source was God; not my job or my bank account. There must be a flow of money coming in and going out. If I was afraid to spend money and held on to it too tightly, I would restrict the flow back to me.

I had so much fear about retirement. It was a growth process since I let go of the role of hospice nurse which brought me many accolades. With this new freedom from working, I was left with many questions. Who am I, now that I am no longer bringing in an income? What was my purpose in life? Will I be okay collecting social security and tapping into my savings and IRAs?

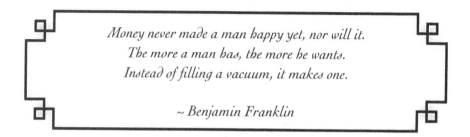

Money never made a man happy yet, nor will it.
The more a man has, the more he wants.
Instead of filling a vacuum, it makes one.

~ Benjamin Franklin

CHAPTER 32

Dorothy's Return

~ ❊ ~

1-26-2011

I wanted to attend Dorothy's memorial service. I called Sandy to inquire about the date and she apologized that she forgot to let me know. It was on January 8th and I missed it.

Sandy told me she wanted to give me Dorothy's book that was just published. We met for breakfast and what a joy it was to see her again! As we thumbed through Dorothy's book and looked at the pictures of her family, we cried and laughed together while sharing memories of her beloved mom. I felt truly connected to Dorothy again.

When I returned home, I decided to read Dorothy's book in my backyard. It contained my favorite Dorothy stories, just as she had read them to me from her unpublished manuscript. I felt Dorothy's presence as I held her book in my hands. She always wanted to become a published author and now she was, thanks to her daughter, Sandy.

3-24-2011

I completed my last shamanic class, the East class, which taught me to face my own death. It was a six-day class and the first three days focused on healing ourselves. This was very powerful work and it was heart wrenching at times.

We did a process where we were able to retrieve the soul essence of someone who died by using our co-leader, Jackie, as a channel. I was lying on my back on a white sheepskin surrounded by my classmates. Incense was burning as Jackie led us in a soul retrieval meditation. I chose to bring back Dorothy, who Jackie said was in the fourth dimension.

Jackie served as the channel for Dorothy's message to me. Dorothy shared she was very happy and that there was life on the other side. I expressed my disappointment that I was not there for her death and she said I was there when I needed to be. She mentioned that she looked forward to every visit with me and how much I helped her. She connected with her loved ones and, most importantly, her son, who had passed away five years before her. She said that it was a very joyous reunion. She alleged, "I knew you were a good witch and that you would find a way to contact me in the afterlife."

I cried throughout the whole process because I felt her presence so strongly. The shaman performed death rites for Dorothy's soul ascension into the light and I felt the release and enormous joy for her.

CHAPTER 33

Chicago Trip for Mother's Day

─── ✻ ───

5-11-2011

While I was in Bali vacationing with my husband, we had a Native American medicine man, Andrew, facilitating our group. I told him about a dream I had and he said that the spirits wanted to give me a message that my mother's transition was very close. I had heard this message two times before from my son and my sister, so I believed it was true. The magic of three meant one should pay attention.

I arrived in Chicago to visit mom for Mother's Day which I thought would be her last one. Mother's Day was pleasant with sunny skies and 70-degree weather. My daughter-in-law, Holly, suggested that we all get together at my sister's house for a potluck. I invited my ex-husband and his wife because he knew that my mother's health was declining and wanted to see her and the family again. It felt good to have us all together and warm feelings flowed all around. Mom did well and enjoyed all of the attention. She had a joyful smile on her face while holding her first great grandchild in her arms, but I noticed how weak she was. She could barely manage the few steps to the bathroom with her walker.

The next day, my dad went to the senior center to play pinochle with his friends. Since the weather was still beautiful, I decided it would be a perfect day to spend with my mom and sister. We went out for breakfast to their favorite place and my mom ate the majority of her meal. Unfortunately, she had the loose bowel situation going on and there were many trips to the bathroom.

Upon returning home, I gave mom a foot massage, which she loved, and I cut her toenails. I performed some Reiki healing and shamanic energy that she always appreciated. She took a nap in her bed and I rested next to her while I cradled her in my arms and felt grateful to be with her.

I had a return flight home on May 12th and decided to cancel it because I wanted to be with my family longer. I intended to enjoy myself with Mom and little Mikey as well as having fun with friends. It was delightful to spend time with my son, Mike, where I have my own room at his condo. I had fun with him and I loved being with my first grandchild. My family was also planning a 90th birthday party for Dad in July. I wondered what life would look like then.

Little Mikey was a total joy in my life with this visit. He had the hiccups and was distressed the other night when I held him after he nursed. I performed Reiki on him with my right hand on his belly and he soon calmed down and stared into my eyes with a blissful look. There was a magical connection that night that I would always remember.

I missed Gary already, but we talked frequently. I was so grateful that he was supportive of my need to be here during my mother's last weeks on earth.

5-12-2011

It was a very special day. My sisters and I decided to meet at our family home to visit with Mom. Angela expressed it was difficult for her to go to Mom's and added that having me there would make it much easier.

When Mom needed to use the bedside commode, I accompanied her and cleaned her up. She stated, "I'm not going to get better. I keep getting worse." At that point, I asked her if she wanted to continue living this way and her response was an adamant "No." I inquired if she was afraid to let go and she said, "Yes." I shared with her that dying was about dropping the physical body and that she would be able to heal the family from the other side and still be around us.

I mentioned hospice again and my mom was more receptive to the idea. She questioned if she would need to leave her home and I assured her that hospice would go to where the patient was. She asked my sisters if they were in favor of it and they agreed that it was the right answer. I was relieved that my sisters would honor my mother's wishes. I communicated to Mom that this was a celebration because she would be graduating to a higher level of being. My mom was spiritual and had seen her angels as well as her spirit guides. She had a connection to the spirit world and was ahead of the game.

We spoke to my dad about hospice and he was in agreement, but he stated, "Let's be positive and not talk about her being terminal." I thought about the saying that "You can't eat an elephant all in one bite." Dad would need some time to adjust to this phase of his life.

CHAPTER 34

Mom on Hospice

~ ✳ ~

I felt honored and blessed to be able to make this trip to Chicago. Mom agreed to give hospice a try for one month after much discussion with her and my two sisters. Most people were not aware that they could initiate hospice for their loved ones by calling hospice and speaking to the admissions team.

I called the Chicago branch of the hospice company that I had worked for. I explained my mother's decline and the factors that made her eligible for hospice: weight loss of 20 pounds in six months; numerous visits to the emergency room for chest pain; and multiple cardiac medications. After contact with her primary doctor, it was agreed that my mother would qualify for hospice care.

The intake nurse arranged a visit to my parents' home when the family would be present in order to hear what hospice had to offer. When they assured Mom that she could give it a try for one month and go back to her home health care if she wanted, she was willing to sign the forms to get hospice started. I confirmed in front of the nurse, who was interviewing my mom, that she could change her mind about hospice. The nurse responded, "Yeah, that's absolutely right. What your daughter said is true. You are free to fire us." That lightened the energy in the room. Mom signed all the required paperwork and hospice started that day.

Hospice brought in the equipment my mom needed: an oxygen-concentrator; portable oxygen; wheelchair; shower chair; walker; and bedside commode. They even provided gloves and diapers along with personal care items. They made available whatever the patient needed, without restrictions, like oxygen saturation values. My dad was delighted for the savings on these personal items as well as the fact that Mom would have a bath aide who would give her a shower and shampoo her hair three times a week.

The hospice nurse would visit twice a week to check mom's vital signs; review and reorder medications; and evaluate how effective her pain medications were. She would receive monthly and as-needed visits from the social worker and chaplain to help her with her emotional and spiritual needs. My dad especially appreciated the 24-hour on-call service that would send someone out to visit Mom in the middle of the night if she got into a crisis, which was usually shortness of breath and chest pain.

Hospice brought in liquid morphine, which was very concentrated, making it easy to administer. They provided an anti-anxiety medication, Ativan, that was a great help for Mom who suffered from anxiety. It was the anxiety that frequently sent her to the hospital and she would go through numerous tests that returned with negative results. I tried to convey that Mom's problem was anxiety-based, but it fell on deaf ears in spite of the fact that they knew I was a nurse.

Hospice saved Medicare millions of dollars by keeping the patient out of the hospital where frequent expensive testing occurred. In my opinion, too much money was spent on end-of-life care that was unnecessary and often painful for patients. I had seen patients agree to aggressive care just to please their loved ones. It was not what the patient wanted and this all came from fear.

The next day, I went to visit Mom again. The equipment company had arrived to deliver her durable medical equipment. The man who delivered the equipment was African American who had a huge spirit. He emanated kindness, compassion and humor. My dad truly connected with him as they shared funny stories and I sat there in awe watching these two men bond. My dad even offered the man some red wine. He poured each of them a drink and they toasted to hospice. That brought a huge smile on my face because I felt something profound had been healed in my father.

I appreciated being with my mother during this time of crisis. I was convinced she was close to making her transition and I wanted to be with her at the time of her death. I did Reiki and shamanic healing for her during my visit and she improved.

I believed Mom was suffering from the side effects of 15 medications. It was helpful that her pulmonologist agreed she was on too many medications and discontinued seven of them. Upon doing my own research, the Statin medication was the most detrimental to her body. She did so much better with less medication.

Mom questioned who would take care of Dad. My sisters told her that they would continue to visit often and bring food. Mom was also concerned about how the bills would be paid. Angela assured her that she would take care of that and had already started doing it, much to my relief.

Mom settled into the comfort of hospice and enjoyed all the attention she received from her daily hospice visits. She absolutely loved her first nurse because this lady was a gem and made it all so good. She would do a complete assessment and give her lots of love by being kind, gentle and caring. The staff assured her she would not need to go back to the hospital. When she became short of breath, there was morphine that would be administered. The combination of morphine and Ativan was helpful in end-of-life care. There was major anxiety in my mother's life due to family dynamics. Luckily, she did quite well because she was getting regular care.

I discovered through my hospice years that no one wanted to talk about the dying process. It was uncomfortable and people thought they were protecting their loved ones. The reality was that when it was brought out into the light and discussed with love and reassurance, magic happened. It cleared the air and everyone would breathe better. It was easier than anyone thought and was a necessary process for the loved one nearing a transition. According to Dr. Ira Byock, in his book *The Best Care Possible,* "Maybe instead of cryo-societies we should develop societies for dealing with the questions of death and dying, to encourage a dialogue on this topic and help people to live less fearfully until they die."

6-7-2011

I had the urge to run away and bury my head in the sand because it was difficult to face some of life's realities, especially those surrounding family conflicts. I was finding out that I would not need to be the strong one all the time. I broke down in tears twice and Angela was there with a warm hug and let me cry. Thank God for my sister.

So much had happened since hospice came into the picture for my mom. They encouraged the families to arrange for funeral/mortuary services and we did that with Dad. We received an estimate and made decisions about prayer cards and verses. I crumbled reading those verses and thank God that Angela was there again for me. This was the verse that we selected for our beloved mother:

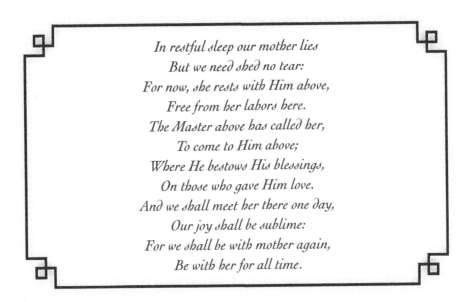

In restful sleep our mother lies
But we need shed no tear:
For now, she rests with Him above,
Free from her labors here.
The Master above has called her,
To come to Him above;
Where He bestows His blessings,
On those who gave Him love.
And we shall meet her there one day,
Our joy shall be sublime:
For we shall be with mother again,
Be with her for all time.

My dad asked the appropriate questions and chose the prayer card that resembled the Greek Orthodox religion. It was funny that he believed that when someone died, it was the end; however, he would uphold the rule that one must be in mourning for 90 days after a loved one passed. I could sense that he was having a hard time with Mom's decline and with the fact that she was terminal. He said he would not want a birthday party on July 23 if she transitioned.

My parents met when my dad was on a short break from the army during World War II. He was in California and did not have the time or money to return home to Chicago. My uncle, Nick, invited him to visit his family home in San Francisco. They were buddies and my dad agreed to follow him home to that house that sat on a hill. That was when he met my mom.

My dad loved to tell the story that it was love at first sight and he knew she was the woman he would marry. They corresponded by mail during the war and my mom savored every letter. When the war ended, my father came for my mother who was waiting for him. They moved to Chicago because that is where my dad found work. They were living with my grandmother when I was born. Things were difficult for my parents during those early years, but they persevered through many trials and tribulations. They celebrated over 60 years of marriage.

My mom often shared with me that I was her angel. She said how happy she was to have a daughter who she could call her own. She was thrilled to have children to love. Mom showed us love in the best way she knew how. I realized that they were both doing the best that they could.

It felt good to get those important decisions completed while Dad was still in denial. I was in denial, too, because lately Mom was doing so well. We picked out a dress for her funeral. We had a great time going through her CDs to find the perfect music and I played the songs she had chosen. I almost broke down when we played her favorite song, "Ave Maria," which I had to stop playing. I treasured these Mondays I had with her, but she knew I planned to return home at the end of June.

Mom asked me to call her life insurance company and we were pleasantly surprised that her death benefit was $27,500. I told her that I would pay the caregiver out of my own funds and that Dad could reimburse me when he received the life insurance. Mom joked, "I'm worth more dead than I am alive." We had a hearty laugh and I told her she was priceless. It was comforting to see my mother feeling energized because she made important decisions about the end of her life.

I was so delighted that Mom was reading *Home with God* by Neale Donald Walsch and *Return to Love* by Marianne Williamson. She expressed they were preparing her for death as was hospice. She said she knew that her angels and loved ones would be there to help her cross over. It was so wonderful that my mom was so spiritual.

Since Mom had all her ducks in a row, I believed she would feel free to transition. My wish for her was a peaceful death and comfort for our family. I chose to send my siblings the link to DyingConsciously. org because it was a comforting resource for those of us preparing for this process.

6-18-2011

It was hard to believe Andrew's statement from spirit that my mom's time was getting closer because Mom was doing very well. She walked around with her walker and went into the fridge to take out food for lunch. Three weeks ago, she could hardly get from the bed to the bedside commode. Was this the peak before dying that I had witnessed so often or the result of the healings I had done for her?

A few days ago, I was able to enjoy my grandson all to myself for three hours. Mikey was a delightful baby and hardly cried. I took him to my friend's house and sat on the grass in Peg's backyard. He put his feet in the grass and felt its coolness. He smiled and cooed a lot. What a precious one! Thank you, God, for all the gifts in my life.

6-23-2011

Andrew was so helpful and asked me if I was "complete" with Mom. I shared that I was about 90% there. The "I love you" part had been completed, but the "I forgive you" part had not. He mentioned that I needed to release her so she could go and that after she passed away, I should take a few of her belongings and bring them home to take to the sweat lodge. Mom would be around us for one year and then we would release her to spirit.

Love and forgiveness were honest conversations that hospice patients and their families needed to have. It could be difficult to start these conversations, but they were so vital because they created an opening and bridged the gaps for each family member. Most importantly, forgiveness was the gift we gave to ourselves. After figuring this all out, the one thing I knew for sure was that my family needed to heal.

6-27-2011

Today was my ex-husband's birthday and I decided to go to his birthday party. I wanted to be with Mike, Holly, and Mikey as they were planning on attending. I chose not to put myself first since I could have enjoyed the day at Lake Katherine.

It was bothering me to be in Chicago this long as it had been difficult. I wanted to go home to Gary, my two cats and my life. Fortunately, I found two 12-step program groups. I found it funny that I was convinced that they did not exist in this area and I was so glad I took the initiative to find them.

I had a dream last night that my mom was much younger with black hair. I was watering a planter and she said I was not doing it right. I got mad and told her, "Then, you do it." I never had the courage to speak up for myself. I seldom needed to do it back home in California because I was surrounded by highly conscious minded people, but I faced challenges here. I even challenged my dad when he could not understand why I did not arrive at the Greek festival on time for Father's Day. I did not feel the need to explain myself although we were late that day because of Mikey's naptime.

I decided to smoke my plant medicine before my visit with Mom. It opened my consciousness so that I could talk freely and I started the conversation about her feelings on dying so that it would complete my time with her. She told me she was not afraid to die, but did not want to leave her family. I reassured her that her soul would remain with us as our guardian angel. I thanked her for being a good mother and that I knew she did the best she could. I forgave her for any hurts and disappointments that still lingered. I felt greater love for my mother as the walls came tumbling down.

On Sunday, I was impressed when I saw my mom's nurse, Margaret. She gave her a morphine shot for her pain and my mother made it clear that she did not want to depend on that. I tried to reassure her that it was okay. Many of my patients expressed a concern about getting addicted to pain medications. I educated them that when medications were used as directed, addiction was not an issue. I never saw addiction as a problem with any of my patients.

7-1-2011

It was a fairly difficult day. I smoked; did some healing work; and sent an email about love to my siblings. I realized that I no longer wanted to be in Chicago; however, I knew I would miss Mike, Holly and little Mikey the most. I wanted to return home to my sweet husband, my adorable cats and the California sunshine. It was a good visit and I accomplished a lot. Mom, Dad and I reminisced about the beauty of our lives looking at pictures and we had a great Mother's Day and Father's Day together.

My dad will turn 90-years-old on July 20th. My sister decided to have a party for him and I was undecided about whether to go. I talked to my good friend, Brigid, and she said that I could decide later about Dad's party depending on what felt right. I tend to be a people pleaser and wanted to put my own needs first.

CHAPTER 35

A Letter to Mikey

~ ❀ ~

Dear Mikey,

You were born April 10, 2011. I wish I could have been there, but I lived 2,000 miles away. You had a plan when you would enter this life on planet earth. Your mom wanted you to be born when your daddy was in town because he traveled three to five days a week. I connected with you and asked you to time your arrival when your dad would be home and you complied. Thank you for that.

I went to Bali with my husband, Gary, from April 8th – 25th. I found out about your mom's trip to the hospital after her water broke through your dad's email to me. The next email said you weren't responding well to the Pitocin and they needed to do a C-section. That concerned me because I could not be there.

I was wide awake at 4:00 a.m. when I was looking through my Facebook account and saw the picture of your dad holding a newborn body in his arms with a huge smile on his face. I started crying tears of joy and Gary was so happy for us. It was a great delight to show that picture to my tour group friends in Bali. They were so happy for me.

You, little Mikey, gave me the gift of your presence to fill my soul with joy and love so that I was able to stay in Chicago for two months, allowing me to see my mother during that time. I had a special day alone with her on Mondays when my dad went to the senior center to play cards. I was able to spend eight hours with your great grandmother. I did the shamanic healing treatment and Reiki on her. Then I massaged her feet, legs and arms.

Your mom and dad took you over to see Great Grandma several times in that two-month period and she showered you with love and kisses. She willed herself to stay alive so she could meet you in person even though her health was declining

During those two months, her condition improved greatly and she was able to get around alone without the walker. She always loved being independent and felt bad when she had to rely on others, so it was good to see the improvement. I left my shamanic beads and crystals under her bed as she slept at night and that energy helped as well.

I was able to see you three to five days a week and I would take you for a walk in the stroller I bought for you. We would go to my friend Peggy's house about four blocks away. She had a beautiful backyard with huge maple trees that provided cooling shade on those hot and humid Chicago summer days. She wasn't home, so I helped myself to her lawn chair. I would hold you, play with you and kiss you for hours.

Thank you, Mikey, for coming into our lives!

CHAPTER 36

Reflections on Life

~ ❖ ~

7-9-2011

I processed a lot since I returned home and was reflecting on all that took place since May 6th. I called my mom while I was at the beach and it was the first time I talked to her since I left Chicago six days ago. I shared with her about my insight that little Mikey gave us the precious gift of his presence so that I could be with her for two months. I told her about the book I had been working on since 1997 about my hospice experiences and she got the shivers. She asked me to send her parts of it so she could look it over and give her input. She mentioned that she would like to add her reflections about what it was like to be a hospice patient and I graciously expressed to her that I would love that.

I had a lot of anxiety about starting to put this book together because it was divided into two notebooks and loose-leaf papers. My husband did the Core Dynamics technique on me regarding this book and I uncovered so many doubts and anxiety about not being good enough. I felt so good after the process and had a deep sense of gratitude that this special man was in my life to support me.

8-30-2011

I meditated outside this morning sitting in our cabana while reading 12-step program material. It felt so good to be home again. I loved being alone and sleeping alone was okay, too. I had been doing it for the last three weeks anyway.

We were still working out the details of getting a caregiver for Mom. I had feelings of anger and frustration when dealing with people and I knew that the answer was love. I needed to trust that God was in charge and that everything would work out in the divine right order.

9-1-2011

It was an extraordinary day! I was resting in bed since 4:30 a.m. and I channeled that I needed to do healing work on myself at 6:00 a.m. for the first hour. That message came to me in June and I did not listen, but I channeled it again and knew I should pay attention to it this time.

I began my day around 6:00 a.m. by listening to Abraham meditation. I smoked; went outside to our cabana; put on Donna De Lory's Remixes; laid down on the mesa cloth; and put Kuyas, my shamanic healing stones, on each of my chakras. I was loving my time alone and the energy was amazing!

On Monday, I decided not to take a bike ride as I wanted time for healing work on myself in our backyard in our lovely cabana. I loved summer and this was my first one since retirement.

I decided not to take Medicare Part B and mailed back their card. My mom paid $256 for three months of insurance and for what? So, they could give her useless antibiotics that destroyed her colon? Now, she had constant diarrhea. She was put on the medicine wheel and I do not want that to happen to me. They would put me on blood pressure pills and I would be focused on what was wrong with me instead of enjoying my life. I would rather spend that money on Heller work, deep tissue bodywork, and a gym. That was where I would find my health – not in tests and pills. They wanted to give healthy people pills so they could make money. My mom was healthy, but she was stressed and filled with anxiety. She was blocked due to fear. She did not have what was available to me. I felt so blessed that I found a holistic path to health.

I thought about Aunt Toni who had a triple bypass surgery which was extremely difficult for her. One year later, she got lung cancer and died a painful death. If she did not have insurance, she would have continued loving her precious Dobermans until the day she was to exit this world from a heart attack. Were we keeping people alive too long so that they ended up with cancer?

I was thinking a lot about death lately. I had watched so many people die in my hospice career. I was also preparing myself for when my time comes. I knew that it involved trusting that something existed on the other side and that was the confirmation from my patients that I received during my hospice years – that life goes on. Death was simply a doorway to something greater. It was like returning the rental car back to Avis and then we go on. This life that we were living was a manifestation of God. We were all playing a role in this amazing play called Life and we were all taking it much too seriously … especially me. Now it was time to kick back and enjoy life. As I continued with my journey, I kept growing and changing.

CHAPTER 37

Healing Work

~ ❋ ~

Cole's mother called me when she saw my ad in a spiritual magazine. Her son had been sexually abused at a daycare center and was acting out. She asked if I would be a good healer for her son by using her body as a pendulum to answer the question. Her body went forward indicating the affirmative. I wanted to help this 10-year-old boy by doing distant shamanic healing on him. I would be healing myself as I healed him.

9-5-2011

Generally, I had no problem getting up, but I was aware that Gary was still in bed and I did not want to wake him. My plant medicine was opening up channels for me and I was more relaxed and centered.

Gary had been home since Friday. I missed my alone time; however, I was able to do my healing work in my Reiki room for an hour and then relaxed in our cabana for meditation while reading my 12-step program books.

I began to feel better since working on Cole. His mother shared with me that she saw a dramatic improvement in him since I started doing distant shamanic healing. He was smiling and laughing a lot. He also picked up his guitar and started playing again. When I checked my chakras this morning, I had two closed; just like Cole. After the session, I checked myself an hour later and we both had all seven of them open. The lesson I learned is that we are all truly One and that what we give out into the world comes back to us multiplied.

CHAPTER 38

Family Dynamics

11-4-2011

I learned to be flexible with people – especially with my loved ones. It was not always an easy thing to do because I had a tendency to want things my way. When I stayed in the higher vibration of love and sought the answers from God, my life unfolded in a beautiful way.

11-18-2011

My oldest son, Tom, celebrated his 40th birthday yesterday. I could not believe I had a child this old and I remembered my mom saying those words to me when I turned 40.

So much happened since I visited my family this past May. That trip was challenging for me because I had to face our family dynamics. I knew I had to walk in the path of love, forgiveness and compassion.

Sam was in my life as one of my greatest teachers. I remembered hearing that the most unlovable person was the one who needed love the most. When he showed up at my parents' home that Monday asking for peace, I knew I had to forgive him. I knew I could not walk around with this veil of resentment around me because that energy would permeate the cells of my body and cause me harm.

I had to do the same with my sister when she was feeling fear. And because I forgave her, I was able to be a part of my nephew's newborn son's life. I looked forward to holding him in my arms. Forgiveness was the gift I gave myself.

I was praying for my family recently. I wanted to spread love and light to the world and it started with my family. I decided to send Sam some sunshine in the form of weekly emails. The emails included a picture of my two cats and a paragraph about their cute antics about the love that they brought to our lives. My wish was that Sam would adopt two kittens. Animals were a great source of unconditional love. My two cats brought me and my husband laughter, joy and love.

CHAPTER 39

Retirement

~ ❋ ~

11-23-2011

Yesterday was my first anniversary of walking into hospice and giving them my resignation notice. I was adjusting to being retired. So much of my identity was wrapped up in being a hospice nurse and I received a lot of kudos in my career. I needed to come to terms that my self-worth was not about the job I had or the amount of money I made. My self-worth came from being who I am and the love I gave to others.

It was so interesting last Sunday when I ran into my former co-worker, Cynthia. I told her that I was retired and she was happy for me. She talked about how the hospice company we both worked for had bad energy and I picked up that energy. I saw truth in that.

I loved the fact that I could sleep-in every morning. I no longer had a job to go to or managers to answer to. I always had to fight off guilt when my manager called to ask if I would work on my day off or to see another patient that day. I learned to say, "No." My days off were crucial to my well-being. Time spent with my husband was more important than overtime pay.

This first year of retirement was one of growth and discovery. I continued with my healing work and I learned to let go of my fears around having enough money. I filled my days with spending time at the ocean, going to lunch with friends and my 12-step meetings where I was of service to several women that I sponsored. We worked the Steps together and I continued to grow through them. I felt truly blessed with this gift called retirement.

Another blessing was being able to have the time to work on this book. It was such a growth process and I wanted to run away from it every chance I could. Gary and I would discuss my book and he liked to remind me that it was work. I did not want it to be work. I wanted it to be the angels doing the work for me. That was what my angel card reading revealed – that I had these angels around me that were assisting me.

I was sitting in my beautiful Reiki healing room, the room that God healed people through my hands, and now I was healing myself. I was healing myself with plant medicine and yoga. I started doing yoga three weeks ago and I already saw phenomenal changes in myself. I was more relaxed and centered and I knew that the plant medicine had a lot to do with it. It was something I had hoped my mother would consider. I mentioned plant medicine to her several times and she had no judgment about it as she heard of the medical benefits from the plant.

CHAPTER 40

Plant Medicine

I chose to become a medical cannabis patient because it was beneficial for my anxiety and depression as well as opening my chakras to divine source energy. During my career as a hospice nurse, I saw the need for this plant medicine, but hospice would not provide it for the patients because it was regulated by Medicare with its Western medical module.

I felt deep sympathy for patients when their medications did not help or the side effects were so severe that taking the medication was not worth it. I encouraged the families to try to get cannabis from other sources. Cannabis helped nausea symptoms as well as pain and anxiety.

In my 30-year career in nursing, I saw many unwanted side effects with pharmaceuticals. Cannabis did not have the disabling side effects that man-made chemicals had. It was a natural herb that the Creator put on this planet for a reason. There was some speculation that it might also kill cancer cells.

> *"It doesn't have a high potential for abuse, and there are very legitimate medical applications. In fact, sometimes Marijuana is the only thing that works… It is irresponsible not to provide the best care we can as a medical community, care that could involve Marijuana. We have been terribly and systematically misled for nearly 70 years in the United States, and I apologize for my own role in that."*
>
> ~ Dr. Sanjay Gupta, Neurosurgeon

I was at a Super Bowl party and one of the gentlemen talked about how distraught his mother was. It was because her youngest son would be in prison for the next 23 years – all because he grew some cannabis in his yard in Nevada. Were we nuts? What were we doing to our children?

Our prisons were overcrowded with those who chose the path of drugs. They took drugs because they were in pain and our country chose to punish them. We spent billions of dollars on the war against drugs with no positive outcome. Plenty of money would be saved if we released the prisoners of drug-related sentences. We could put that money into education for our children by teaching them about the pitfalls of drug use. We did not need to build more jails. We are our brother's keepers and we are all in this together as one.

Our children needed to be loved and nourished. They needed our kindness and compassion because they went through tough times in their lives, including family crises and peer pressure. They were dealing with the violence that was abundant in our culture and I admired the strong family connections that I witnessed during my travels to other countries. Our country needed more of that instead of isolation. Our children could change the world into a better place than how they found it.

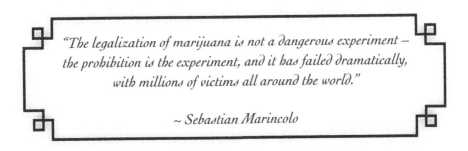

"The legalization of marijuana is not a dangerous experiment – the prohibition is the experiment, and it has failed dramatically, with millions of victims all around the world."

~ Sebastian Marincolo

Haven't we learned anything through the prohibition fiasco? The government should not be able to legislate a person's choice in how they wanted to live their lives. We needed to let people live as they wanted, without interference from a fear-based government that sent its young men to war to fight some unknown brothers.

Cannabis became illegal because the hemp production was a huge threat to the lumber industry. The reason that happened was because it was also a threat to Mr. Big Bucks, also known as corporations. There was this conspiracy that if they kept people stupid, they could control them. What was not understood was there was a need for this plant medicine for medical purposes and, therefore, cannabis should be legalized with the criminal aspect taken out of it.

The thing about cannabis being used as plant medicine is that it is legal in some states and not in others. It reminded me of the war of the South and the North in the early days of America. The people of the North thought it was inhumane to keep slaves and not give people their freedom. We went to war over it and many lives were lost. Just like the lyrics in a song "War – what is it good for? Absolutely nothing."

My belief was that all drugs should be legal. Let people do what they wanted. If we calculated all the money spent on the war against drugs and put it into greater causes, what a different world we would be living in! Those funds could go to helping one another from the pain of living and dying in a society that isolated itself from one another.

In my opinion, cannabis was better than alcohol. I saw so much harm from alcohol – liver cancer was one of them as was cirrhosis of the liver. Truth be told, the body was not made to handle alcohol. It destroyed so many lives, and yet, we made it legal because a profit would be made. Corporations taxed it and the greed kept growing, but the emptiness within never would be filled with money.

In my life, I had to face my fears around scarcity consciousness. I held on to money for dear life with a closed fist because I was raised by parents who preached saving for a rainy day. It served me well in some aspects, such as establishing a savings plan for retirement. But now that I was in the twilight of my years, I was learning to let go of the money and putting it to good use by helping others.

Being of service was connecting to that higher power. It was time to stop this senseless war on drugs and do what was right for the people. We had somebody like Oprah who was out there living her life and brought us quality television shows about spirituality. She had passion in her eyes and a message she gave to us all. She opened the way for all people to step into their power. She was my heroine.

Whenever there was a problem, the answer would always be love – no exceptions. It was time for all of us to get back to love. The world would be a better place if we replaced fear with love. Fear was just another word for war and war came from fear that there was not enough to go around; therefore, we hoarded for ourselves while others suffered. We were all looking for love. Plant medicine enhanced that love because it connected me to the divine.

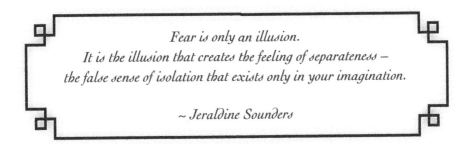

Fear is only an illusion.
It is the illusion that creates the feeling of separateness –
the false sense of isolation that exists only in your imagination.

~ Jeraldine Sounders

CHAPTER 41

Alternative Medicine

I faced my own death every day because I was not part of a medical plan. When my Medicare card came in the mail, I had the option of signing the back of the card and stating that I did not want Medicare Part B which covered medical doctors, diagnostic tests and lab work. Medicare Part A covered hospitalization and services, home health, hospice and skilled days in nursing homes.

After being in the medical field as a Registered Nurse for the past 30 years, I lost faith in the Western Medical module except for crisis care and ER expertise and I was especially against pharmaceuticals. After much prayer and meditation, I signed the back of the card and sent it back to Medicare. My card reads "Medicare Part A only." It was not about the money because I could well afford my social security to be cut to $1,550 from the $1,700 to be paid for this premium. I heard people talking about Medicare being "free," but the reduction in their social security payment paid for their premium.

I chose alternative medicine to keep me healthy. I was spending money on myself with weekly acupuncture treatments; monthly chiropractic treatments; Heller bodywork; Kundalini yoga; and massage to heal two herniated disks. My disk injury was a blessing in disguise in many ways as it led me to a Chinese doctor who performed acupuncture along with Chinese herbs. It taught me to receive help which was always difficult for me.

My Chinese doctor told me about one of his clients who had six back surgeries with no relief from his pain. This client's doctor referred him to my acupuncturist and he was finally free from back pain. It was a shame that he did not find the Chinese doctor first.

I was thinking of a story about a gentleman whose family took him to the doctor for various problems and they diagnosed him with cancer. The family felt it would be in his best interest not to tell him he had cancer that was inoperable. The doctor predicted that his life expectancy would be six months and the gentleman lived a robust 10 years. I believed he lived that long because he did not put his energy into that diagnosis and focused on his health. I always believed that what we put our focus on would materialize.

I decided not to have another mammogram because I did not want to live in fear. I did not want a problem to be found that could be cured with Chinese herbs and acupuncture. Instead, I chose to be in gratitude for my good health and put my focus there.

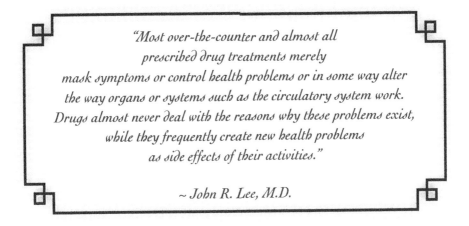

"Most over-the-counter and almost all
prescribed drug treatments merely
mask symptoms or control health problems or in some way alter
the way organs or systems such as the circulatory system work.
Drugs almost never deal with the reasons why these problems exist,
while they frequently create new health problems
as side effects of their activities."

~ John R. Lee, M.D.

CHAPTER 42

Blessings of Being a Hospice Nurse

~ ❄ ~

1-2-2012

There were many blessings in my career, but there were also many frustrations. Part of the frustration of being a hospice nurse was the schedule and the fact that I had to be on-call. That would be tough sometimes when I wanted to spend time with my family and pursue other goals. However, the gifts were many and the richness of experiencing death was what helped me come to my own inner belief that death was an illusion.

We were truly eternal beings – we were spiritual beings having a human experience. That was my journey and continued to be my journey as I watched my mother decline while she was on hospice. I was so blessed that she had the support of hospice and that made me feel positive because I knew they were helping her prepare for her transition.

The most enlightening benefit of being a hospice nurse was helping patients prepare for the inevitable by sharing my experience, strength and love. I talked to people honestly and when they asked me a question, I gave them an answer. It was unfortunate that they did not receive that humanness from their doctors because nobody wanted to talk about death. Their questions went unanswered until hospice came along because we were real with them and shared what to expect. We kept them informed about all the steps along the way so they knew what to look for. They would not have to reside in a place of fear because we gave them knowledge. We also encouraged our patients to fill out an advanced directive so that their desires for end-of-life care would be honored by their loved ones.

Hospice empowered family members to keep their loved ones comfortable with the use of morphine and Ativan. These were great medications for short-term use, but I certainly would not recommend them for long-term when there were natural options like plant medicine. Patients could have benefited from an alternative medication, like cannabis, and it was a shame to keep this from dying patients. It was a real crime that people had to suffer needlessly when we had a natural medication that was given to us from God.

Hospice was a satisfying job in so many ways because I met so many incredible people. I loved the freedom of visiting my patients on my schedule with no one looking over my shoulder because my focus was on their well-being.

When Medicare started overseeing hospice, that was when the fear set in. The fear started at the top and filtered down to the staff. The office was more focused on whether paperwork was correct and submitted on time. If a patient's paperwork was not correct, Medicare denied payment for that patient. The bottom line at our company was about revenue and keeping the stockholders happy with healthy profits. It became toxic and that was why I left hospice. I loved the patients and families; however, I could not tolerate working in Corporate America anymore.

1-3-2012

The writing of this book was so intriguing because it allowed me to look at my hospice days in a different light. I thought about all of the different patients I had along the way; all the lessons I had learned; and all of the amazing people I had met. I was reminded of all the negativity and pain that I absorbed because I am an empath. It became apparent that healing myself would become a necessary daily ritual and that led me to the path of spiritual healing and Reiki since I was in such pain.

I took my first Reiki class in 2006 and after my first class, I became in tune to the energy. I realized that I had all of these hospice patients whom I could practice on. I saw what Reiki did for my hospice patients and I became a Reiki master in 2008. I started teaching Reiki and it has been such a remarkable journey.

My hospice days were fulfilling when I reflected back on them. I treasured feeling the love that was present when I walked into the homes and witnessed the family around the patient. I was involved in the dynamics of family members and what they were going through. I was humbled knowing that I was there for them – I was a listening ear; I held their hand; and I gave them a warm embrace. I knew I could not fix it and I surrendered to the will of God. It was a comforting reminder to live life fully; it always started with love and it ended with love because love was all there was.

The most difficult visits were seeing patients in nursing homes because their families were not there. Most of the nurses hated going into nursing homes because we felt the isolation of our patients. We also felt the anguish of the families dealing with the guilt of having to place their loved one in a nursing home because they tried and tried, but for whatever reason, they were not able to provide for them at home. I had to remind myself that everything was in divine right order and it took the pain away because I was not in control.

1-5-2012

Things went well when I lived from the heart. When I lived in a place of love and surrendered my will, I accepted the outcome. This whole journey about letting go of money was huge for me and quitting my hospice job assisted in my healing. I knew I was holding on to the money and security. Most importantly, it was also the medical benefits that came with my job and I struggled with the fact that I would be giving that up. My husband was a contract worker and did not have medical coverage without my policy. I was conflicted because I was not happy with the company, but I knew it was time to let go of thinking that my job was my source instead of God.

CHAPTER 43

Benefits of Cannabis

~ ✦ ~

I smoked some cannabis in the afternoon before I was ready to go home from the end of my shift. A puff was the answer because it helped to calm and clear my mind. I was looking forward to a walk in the park and reflected on the benefits of cannabis.

I have been smoking cannabis for 15 years and had a lot of guilt about it. The first time I tried it was when my friend came to visit and I was about 30-years-old and she was 20-years-old. She offered me a puff and I decided to try it. I began to feel the effects and felt out of control. Then, I was really paranoid and thought, "Oh, My God! What was my husband going to think if he saw me this way? He was going to be really upset with me." I felt guilty and reminded myself that I would be okay. I just let go of everything, including my life, because the greatest fear of all was that I would be annihilated and I knew that was not true.

I discovered I had Attention Deficit Disorder (ADD) and I never wanted to look at that. I tried Ritalin from a friend because I thought it would give me lots of energy, but it was quite the opposite. I tried the Sativa strain of cannabis that was recommended for ADD because it worked on brain chemistry. I found that it cleared my mind, calmed me down and helped me to focus so that I could get things done in a very relaxed and efficient manner. It made me happy to be able to take a natural substance. I discovered that I had developed pretty strong coping skills due to my people pleasing which brought me to terms with who I was. Learning that was part of my spiritual journey with cannabis.

1-8-2012

I firmly believed that so many patients could have been helped with medical cannabis. Over the years of watching people die, I would never forget the young 45-year-old woman with three small children who had cancer. The morphine was not working for her and we kept increasing it, but she was still in pain. It was so difficult to watch her because I felt helpless that I could not help her. Cannabis could have been the answer for her, especially the CBD oil which was the concentration of the medicinal component without the heady effects. It could have possibly given her comfort at the end of her life. That was what cannabis did for some people – it connected them to the source energy so that healing could take place. It was a healing herb that was on this planet for centuries and put here by God for a reason.

One of my patients, Loretta, had horrible nausea. Hospice tried every single medication they could think of and could not get rid it. She tried drinking 7Up and that did not work. Ginger tea could have helped because it was a natural remedy and grew on Mother Earth. It was known that cannabis was an incredible anti-nausea medication for cancer patients and worked wonders, so I never understood why it was not available to non-cancer patients.

When I mentioned cannabis to Loretta's husband, he was so excited because he was well aware of the medicinal purposes. He told me he used to smoke it with his mom who grew it in the backyard. Unfortunately, Loretta could not smoke it because she had a lung problem and could not handle it in that form.

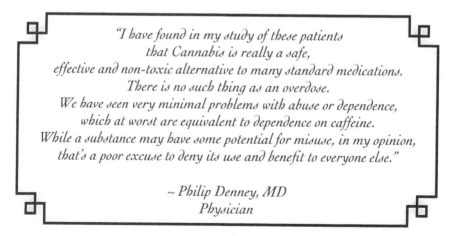

"I have found in my study of these patients
that Cannabis is really a safe,
effective and non-toxic alternative to many standard medications.
There is no such thing as an overdose.
We have seen very minimal problems with abuse or dependence,
which at worst are equivalent to dependence on caffeine.
While a substance may have some potential for misuse, in my opinion,
that's a poor excuse to deny its use and benefit to everyone else."

~ Philip Denney, MD
Physician

CHAPTER 44

Love

~ ❖ ~

Love always showed up in my life in many different ways. One way was through my friends. My friend, Sherry, was doing Reiki on me the other day and I felt my walls starting to crumble down. I felt the love from the divine during that Reiki treatment. I needed to get Reiki from her every week and I would do that by bartering with her.

1-12-2012

I was preparing for my mother's death and felt a deeper love for her as I learned to let go of my judgments. I knew there was work that needed to be done on my part as well as her part. I believed that was why she did not make her transition in May.

I was working on complete forgiveness for how my parents raised me. I realized they did the best they could with the knowledge that they had. My mother was being healed on some level and thank God she lived long enough to meet her two great grandsons, Mikey and Dominick. Dominick was born this past October and Mikey was born in April. My mother was filled with joy when she held them and it was wonderful to witness that love.

I knew that I had to let go of my mother's physical body because it was just falling apart. When I spoke with her yesterday, she complained about her chest pain. I was concerned because she was also having numbness down her arm. She said it was due to her circulation problem and not a heart attack. I, too, have circulation problems and yoga provided relief for that.

Now that I was retired, I was taking money out of my retirement account at a faster rate than my financial advisor recommended. I wanted to live an abundant life in the twilight of my years and decided to follow my heart by enjoying the money that I saved.

I was learning to love myself and I knew that I needed to keep letting go of all the hurt from the past and to trust that God was my source.

1-18-2012

Another way that love showed up in my life was through yoga. My husband and I decided to attend a week-long yoga retreat in Mexico that was fantastic! We stayed at a beautiful resort that was steps away from the ocean. We had the pleasure of meeting some awesome people who shared the love of yoga and spiritual growth. We began each day with vinyasa yoga with Sadie Nardini and our afternoons were free to do as we wished. In the evening, we enjoyed a wonderful vegetarian meal and then came together for a workshop.

I felt grateful that we had the time and means to vacation together at beautiful locations and to share wonderful memories with like-minded people. I had a spectacular massage at the resort from a beautiful woman who was a healer. She told me that I was depressed because I took on the pain and grief of my hospice patients and their families. I recognized the truth in that and she did some energy work to remove some of that pain. I felt much lighter after the session.

During my hospice years, some families shared about a child that crossed over and the enormous pain it caused for all the family members. It was heartbreaking to hear their stories because there were times when I entertained that fear about losing one of my two sons. I was always grateful that my sons were alive and would think about them to connect with them on a spiritual level. There was no separation between those we loved; whether on the earth plane or in heaven.

I learned so much about myself from this trip. It was about letting go and trusting. I thought about all the fear surrounding death that seemed so prevalent in our society. Fortunately, the flip side of fear will always be love.

A 12-step program is about love and support and I go where the love is. This was a beautiful day because it started with my favorite meeting on the beach. I always learned so much from my fellow 12-step program friends. I listened to their stories and related to the commonality we all shared. I have learned that there is a higher power who loves me and watches over me. It was good to have this time of solitude and reflection. Being at the beach was a great place to connect with the divine.

This past year was filled with healing from the pain I acquired from my hospice patients and families. I knew I took on a lot of dense energy and the ocean was where I liked to come to cleanse it all away because saltwater was magical for eradicating negative energy. Walking in the wet sand was like receiving a reflexology treatment because it triggered the points in the foot and was very healing. I practiced self-love by taking this time to be at the ocean. When I gave this time to myself, I had much more to give to others. It was difficult to put my needs first, but I was making great progress in that direction.

I felt very blessed to live in Southern California, even though my family lived in Chicago. I loved visiting, but I was happy I no longer lived there anymore. I could send love to my family and be love when I was with them. When I chose love, I was at my happiest as it symbolized being free. This was something I preached to the caregivers of my patients and some followed my suggestion and others did not. I instinctively knew I needed to follow it, too.

An army helicopter just flew by and I thought about war and how it never solved anything. Our society believed we had to defend our country against another because they were the bad guy. We believed in duality and the notion of, "It's me against the rest of the world," when in reality, we were all one. We were determined to put up walls and barriers because the bottom line was we were afraid of death and it was just another reminder of fear.

We were all droplets in the ocean of love because we came from the same source energy. Whenever there was a problem, the answer was always love because love was what created us. There were really only two things that were real: fear and love.

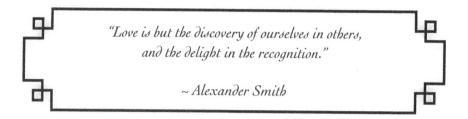

"Love is but the discovery of ourselves in others, and the delight in the recognition."

~ Alexander Smith

CHAPTER 45

Pain Medications

The Enneagram defines 9 personality types. I am a number 6 and there are different levels for the number 6. The top level was being courageous and I thought about my journey thus far.

I found that I gained a great deal of courage in order to speak my truth in all of my encounters – with myself, my husband, my children, my friends and my patients. There were many times I felt conflicted working in a Western Medicine environment when my belief was in natural healing processes. It took an immense amount of courage to share my views with others which was another reason why I chose to write this book.

I called my brother, Sam, and shared with him that I was sorry that I did not respond sooner to his email in regards to our mother's health. We were on vacation and it took a while to catch up with everything. I wanted to let him know how wonderful it was that he visited Mom on Mondays and how it made a difference for her. Sam confided that she appeared confused because all the caregivers told her different things about pain control and medication. Fortunately, I reassured him that it was pretty normal as each caregiver had their viewpoint. What was most important was that Mom needed to determine what was right for her based on how she felt.

With hospice patients, people believed we had all the answers. We thought it was called morphine, but not everyone could handle that. It reminded me of one of my patients named Ken who was very special to me. He was one of the very first patients I saw on hospice. He had this terrible bone cancer and was in a lot of pain. We tried different pain medications, but nothing seemed to work. I felt terrible that he suffered so much. He even asked me to assist him in ending his life. I would not do that since I would not even know how to do so. After all, I was not God.

People should not suffer, especially when there was plant medicine that worked so well. I remembered one day when Gary was feeling really awful and was in so much pain. He decided to indulge in the Indica strain of cannabis and it helped him. His pain was at a level eight and went down to a level one. So, what was that all about and why did we allow people to suffer? It was the same with people that experienced nausea where no amount of medication made a difference. It was all about not going the Western Medicine route – the cut, burn and poison route. It truly was not for me because I saw so much and it all came down to the fear of death. Everybody was running away from it and I chose not to run.

I encouraged hospice patients to look within to find out what was right for them. Sometimes, a full-dose of a medication was too strong and a half-dose worked just fine. I saw the inadequacies of Western Medicine in pharmaceuticals. There were benefits in short-term care in hospice because a patient could take MS Contin twice a day which was a slow-released morphine. That worked pretty well for most people since they were facing the end of their lives and the toxicity that built as a by-product from those medications was not a big deal. However, for long-term use, who really wanted all those toxins in their body? They were man-made chemicals that the body could not assimilate in a healthy way.

Plant medicine was a different story. Nobody ever died from a cannabis overdose – nobody. Even with edibles that could be potent, people would drift off to sleep in a feeling of well-being. They did not get into fights, they did not get drunk and they did not drive in a car and kill somebody else. People did not kill other people on cannabis. People did not run red lights. When they came to a stop sign, they were more likely to sit there until it turned green. Ha! That was what it was like to experience cannabis. It put me in a peaceful state, took away my anxiety and removed the barriers that I put up. It washed away all the layers of soot, like being sprayed by a wonderful shower of love. That was what plant medicine provided for me … a place of peace, stillness and love.

We needed to change the world. People needed to have plant medicine available to them since God provided it. The problem was that cannabis could not be synthesized into a drug as a chemical form. Attempts were made with Marinol and it was not successful with the patients that I visited. So, that told me the drug companies could not use it because they could not replicate it. Plant medicine had to be in its natural form. That meant there was no money to be made for the pharmaceutical companies that were killing people with their chemicals. On the flip side, I did witness Western Medicine that helped many people as there were some pharmaceuticals that were beneficial to patients. However, I strongly felt that the chemicals fed into people's fear and prolonged death because there was no understanding that we were part of the oneness.

It was time to walk into the light of divinity – the light that told me what was right. It was time to open up to the divine wisdom because I would not look to the government for the answers to my life. I started looking within because the answers were there. I had seen what pharmaceuticals did to my mom and my patients and I did not want any part of that. Instead, I chose natural medicine and visited my chiropractor/naturopath.

I observed that our yoga community had no judgment about the use of plant medicine. They looked upon it medicinally because it grew naturally and was put here by God as a healing plant. Besides the medicinal purposes, my experience was that this plant opened the channels to our higher consciousness. The higher-self knew God and was connected to that God energy in wholeness. Maybe that was why the government kept plant medicine illegal in order to keep us in a lower vibration.

Yogi Bhajan stated that the use of pharmaceuticals lowered one's vibration. I had no doubt that this was true. I was so grateful that he brought Kundalini yoga to the West in 1968. This practice broadened my horizons to higher spiritual realms and changed my life in ways I never dreamed possible. It brought my husband and I closer because we were on this path together and we engaged in more honest and heartfelt conversations.

"The evidence is overwhelming that marijuana can relieve certain types of pain, nausea, vomiting and other symptoms caused by such illnesses as multiple sclerosis, cancer and AIDS – or by the harsh drugs sometimes used to treat them. And it can do so with remarkable safety. Indeed, marijuana is less toxic than many of the drugs that physicians prescribe every day."

~ Dr. Jocelyn Elders, MD, Former US Surgeon General
"Myths About Medical Marijuana,"
Providence Journal, March 26, 2004

CHAPTER 46

Gratitude

─── ❄ ───

2-1-2012

Wow, my plant medicine was expanding me in ways that I could only imagine! I was really opening up to the path that spirit was showing me. It was helping me let go of all of society's nonsense and to channel that which I was supposed to channel. I chose not to worry about what it was going to look like in book form because this was my story and I was telling it like it was.

What I have learned was that life was all just a story that I told myself – about this relationship or that relationship or a tragic thing – and that was where I would put my attention. Would the choice be on gratitude to say thanks for all that was around me and thanks for all the blessings? I decided to choose this for my life – to be in the moment of those blessings and to feel the gratitude. It was about being in continual gratitude for all the things that were in my life. When I remained in gratitude, I was able to live in the moment which was the best gift of all.

I felt blessed to be sitting in the cabana in our beautiful yard while I was reading *Wild Love – Kissed into Consciousness* by Dreaming Bear. This was what really stood out for me … "In the interest of staying open, I displayed my heart in a prominent place in my life out in the accessibility of being known." Wow! I read that sentence over and over and realized that it was my opening up and being known that would be my journey.

Cannabis allowed me to be known and to stop hiding who I really was. I let go of the fear of judgment when I told people my story that I used plant medicine and yoga to heal myself. It was similar to a friend who healed herself of panic attacks and agoraphobia by using plant medicine and yoga. She was part of a spiritual community that used plant medicine to get to higher states of consciousness. It was introduced as medicine and not as a drug. Yoga was instrumental to surrendering by utilizing deep breathing, chanting and postures to facilitate the opening up of the chakras.

I am learning who I am through love and authenticity. Dreaming Bear said, "Being authentic is the new cool." It was our fears that kept us from it. Being authentic was about facing fear and walking through it while coming out on the other side and realizing there was nothing there.

I was forever thankful that I had the means to take good care of my health. I kept myself healthy with Heller work each month which concentrated on the deep connective tissues. Most importantly, it was crucial to my well-being that I had an hour of meditation every morning. I began with my plant medicine which gave me a sense of well-being where I was happy and focused. I often felt the angels all around my room helping me to heal. I was getting things done without the anxiety I used to encounter. I would not need to take Ativan for anxiety because long-term use led to higher doses and could also be addictive which was not a pretty picture.

I was very appreciative when I had my plant medicine in Peru as it opened me up to God. It was not about another person who was going to make me happy or thinking that everything would be fine because I was with this person. It was not the truth. It was about looking for myself where I was not – this illusion that when I found my other half, I would become whole. That was a distraction from stepping into my power and into the essence of my true, authentic self.

When I visited Bali, it felt wonderful to partake in a whole different type of plant medicine – mushrooms. It was fascinating to know there was no judgment against it. What a freeing concept! That was why the people of Bali were so happy. They could partake in this plant God put on the earth to assist in connecting to the divine power and remove unwanted blockage. The people living in Bali also spent time in prayer and devotion every day and it was a joy to witness their rituals.

I was grateful I stepped beyond fear and made the decision to travel to Peru in December 2009. I experienced a deep spiritual journey with the use of plant medicine that grew through cactus plants. San Pedro is a very sacred, ancient cactus that has been a part of continuous healing tradition in Peru for over 3000 years. Plant medicine was legal in Peru and there were no senseless laws that put people in jail for expanding their consciousness through magical plants. Their ceremonies were about honoring and giving blessings for the plant as well as opening up to the plant's message. My enlightening experience was of merging with the divine and I knew beyond a doubt that I was a part of the oneness. I felt overwhelming love, joy and peace that I know will await me when my time comes to make my transition.

2-2-2012

I was so fortunate to be sharing time with Gary in our cabana and reading *Wild Love* by Dreaming Bear. I truly resonated with this – "I bow to everything as my Beloved because everything becomes God again in the end." Each morning, I would begin by listening to his CD *Transluminal Flux* while I was doing yoga after having my plant medicine. All the spirit guides were there helping me to heal. This book has unlocked higher levels of consciousness for me and I was eternally grateful!

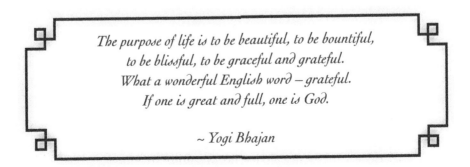

The purpose of life is to be beautiful, to be bountiful,
to be blissful, to be graceful and grateful.
What a wonderful English word – grateful.
If one is great and full, one is God.

~ Yogi Bhajan

CHAPTER 47

More Reflections on Life

~ ❄ ~

2-3-2012

My adventure in Bali was astounding! Gary and I laid on a beanbag under this beautiful overhanging tree while soaking up the beauty of the aquamarine ocean and white sand beach. I let go of spending $5000 on this cabana and it was worth every single penny. I experienced oneness and felt so connected. I knew without a doubt, I was part of the divine energy that I liked to call source energy. For me, the energy of love and nature consisted of source energy.

I learned to take care of my needs and everything was so much better for my family. I became much more relaxed when I was able to indulge in my plant medicine and surrendered the anxious mom who tried to control everything.

2-5-2012

I needed to surrender this dream I was living and the shamanic way was to open up with the use of plant medicine. I was told that when cannabis was taken after having the experience of San Pedro, the cannabis reactivated the San Pedro for additional healing and spiritual connection.

I was raised in such a strict family with so much shame, guilt and prejudice. I could not figure out where the pain came from. I had blocked so much out to protect myself and walked around with this shame and guilt. I wanted to step out from the fear of my life and stir up some lives.

I want my book to become controversial. I had a story to tell and this was going to come out. I knew it was a story that needed to be told because our patients needed natural medication. The nausea I have seen … Oh, My God, so much nausea. My patients trying pill after pill and nothing worked – even the really expensive one, Zofran. None of those medications worked. But, cannabis worked! It should be celebrated and legalized so that people would not have to go through so much pain and nausea when nearing the end of their lives.

We needed to legalize all drugs. Let people live the way they wanted to live – free and without restrictions, rules and laws. What the world needed was to love one another; embrace one another; and accept one another for who we are. We should open our hearts; talk to each other; and connect with each other. I learned so much from others.

I had a conversation with a woman who had atrial fibrillation and the medications did not work. She had surgery twice in 2006 and that did not work. She was still on the medications. What if cannabis could have helped this woman with her condition? There were so many people living with various illnesses; including epilepsy, cancer and Alzheimer's that cannabis could help.

I found that the masses were all afraid of death and kept returning to the doctor so death would not prevail. The problem was that most medications did not work. Companies were happy to take the money, but they did not have the answer to life. The answer was in letting go of all of one's fears. Plant medicine was teaching me this truth.

2-6-2012

Was it so bad to die? I was totally cool with the fact that I do not know what my blood pressure is. Both my parents were on medication for high blood pressure, but that was not for me. My two sisters had breast cancer. It was one of the scariest things to have a mammogram and then wait for the results. Well, you know what? I chose not to put my energy there and believed in my healing work. I found out that cannabis was very good for breast cancer. However, my sister lived in Illinois where it was not legal. Why don't we just legalize it?

The world just needed to wake up! Let people do what they needed to do to allow them to live without pain, anxiety and many other conditions. We needed to love each other instead of condemning each other for our choice of medication. Why were we making them wrong? I knew I was not doing anything wrong because I was helping and healing myself and that was so profound.

Kundalini yoga helped me break down the walls that I built around myself with the guidance of my healing angels that visited me. It taught me to plunge deeper into my seven chakras which were the energy centers of my body. Yoga cleared all the chakras so the energy flowed through. It was a great practice on so many levels and it helped with my strength and flexibility. It was time for me to step into my power.

2-7-2012

Why would it take so long for change to occur when it was evident that it should be about unity, love and mutual respect for one another? It should not matter what our skin color, age, or status is, or how much money was in the bank; we were all equal.

My 12-step program taught me not to be in judgment. I saw the judgment in myself and by recognizing it, I could transform it – as long as I would not run away from it. If I stepped into the fear and into the feeling, I knew that God was guiding me. That was what my 12-step program was all about: my favorite slogan – *Let Go and Let God*.

We all have a connection to the divine source and it made us interconnected. We needed each other, but we needed each other in love and unity – not this narrow vision of always being right and saying others were wrong. It was a matter of perspective; a matter of how people were raised. Our parents were raised a certain way and they passed down their beliefs to their kids, so as children we were innocent victims.

I was able to have a greater compassion for others because of my hospice career. But, I needed to have compassion and love for myself first. I kept affirming to myself that I was whole, perfect and complete just the way I was. I knew that it was all in divine right order. It was about being co-creators in the world and co-creators with our divine source; you know, that God bliss. It was time to unite people, recognize the oneness and take care of each other with long hugs. We needed to walk a mile in another man's moccasins to truly understand his path.

2-8-2012

I always did my best to keep the light when others panicked because there was nothing to fear. There should be no fear of death because we are part of the one that is called God, Buddha, Hare Krishna, or whatever. It was the energy that kept the planets in orbit. It was love, love, and love! When I could be in a place of love, I was at my best.

My plant medicine enriched me with so much awareness. It was connecting me to the divine energy and helping me to understand my life at a higher vibration. I was so aware of my judgmental attitude toward others and of the critical voice that kept harping away at me that I was not good enough. The time came for sweet-talking myself about how beautiful I was on the inside and the outside. Self-esteem was the last hurdle on my way to enlightenment. I was raised in the mass consciousness of not being good enough and it came from generations of the past. Feeling that I was not good enough made me do all kinds of things to put salve on the wound.

Love is the answer to any problem in life. Think about a problem you have been dealing with. Then think, *Love is the answer*. Really get your mind around that. What would that feel like to you? What would it be like to surround the situation with love?

People had so many different views about what lies beyond this life after death. For most people, it was heaven or their version of it. I remembered a man who did not believe there was anything beyond and that made me wonder. It was what prompted me to ask my favorite patients to come back to me and give me a sign that would be obvious. I was so thrilled to receive these messages from the afterlife.

I was still in communication with my long-term patient, Carolyn, who had suffered from pulmonary fibrosis for the past six years while on hospice. She loved the distant Reiki I gave her every morning and I had beautiful visions during her sessions. Her daughter said she would call me when Carolyn was close to making her transition so I could be at her side. I was not there for Lil, but perhaps I could be there for Carolyn. Carolyn told me that she and I will always be connected and I believed that.

2-9-2012

I have always admired Carolyn's daughter as she took care of her mom 24/7. I don't know how she did it and I doubt that I could be that selfless. My mother was on hospice and it was my 90-year-old dad who was caring for her. I lived 2,000 miles away, so it was impossible for me to be her caregiver. I also knew it was not what I wanted to do. In fact, I told my kids that if I ever needed full-time care, they should put me in a home and continue to live their lives. I would not want to be a burden to my family.

The other day, my gifted friend, Sherry, channeled my aunt Toni who had a message for me that she was at the beach as I was writing my book. I felt her presence at the beach. Aunt Toni was a pistol and a lot of fun, but she was a smoker. She had a heart attack and her doctor convinced her to have open-heart bypass surgery for her blocked arteries and her recovery was long and difficult. One year later, she found out that she had lung cancer that had spread to other organs. She went through chemotherapy and radiation to no avail and she suffered a painful death. If she would not have had the heart surgery, she would have continued living out her life with her beloved Dobermans and her passion for dog shows. Her experience taught me that I did not want to go the Western Medical route. I believe we all have a time to die, but it was the fear of death that made us seek out medical care to prolong our life.

2-10-2012

I enjoyed a beautiful day in Laguna Beach. I struck up a conversation with a woman my age about my book and the use of medical cannabis for patients. She shared a story with me about her brother who had stomach pain for many years with no relief from the various pharmaceuticals he used. In desperation, he tried medical cannabis that worked well and allowed him to enjoy his meals pain-free. We talked about how this medicine needed to be openly available without the stigma. Our people were suffering while we had overblown military defense budgets. We needed to care for each other and love one another. We needed to put our money into a society that worked for the people.

CHAPTER 48

Lessons I Learned From Hospice

~ ❊ ~

2-11-2012

Some of the greatest advice I received from my hospice patients was to live for today and not put my life on hold for some magical day in the future when I retired. I met so many patients who had saved for their retirement and bought an RV to travel, only to have those plans changed due to a serious illness.

My many years in hospice gave me countless lessons about human behavior – specifically at the end of life. There was a lot of fear for the patient and family members when death approached. The person dying was a reminder to the family of their own mortality which was something most people avoid thinking about. I saw an abundance of devotion from family members who stayed by the side of their loved ones. I witnessed that devotion in my 90-year-old dad as he was the primary caregiver for my 89-year-old mother. My parents were married over 60 years and it was very difficult for them to face the reality of losing one another. They chose denial to cope and that was okay for them.

I was so grateful that my father went out twice a week to the senior center to play cards with his friends because it kept him sane. I often told my hospice families how important it was to fill their cups first by taking care of their own needs. Some would listen, but others did not and suffered burnout. Who was I to judge their path?

There were also many miracles that occurred during the dying process. It was this ultimate sacred space that was created with the divine and led us through the passage into love and bliss. Death was an illusion because we never were born and neither would we die. We were eternal spiritual beings having a human experience.

2-23-2012

I was thinking a lot about death and losing someone that I loved. I knew my mother's time was close and I did not know when it would be. I could get into fear so easily. When fears came up for me, I learned to return to the breath. Kundalini yoga taught me to breathe deeply and exhale completely to release my fears. I did my best to remember this when fear would rear its ugly head. Kundalini yoga has been in my life for a month now and made such a difference.

2-24-2012

I learned another lesson from hospice about equal opportunity for all. We would admit non-funded patients if they had no insurance or means to pay. Equal opportunity was brought to light by a movie I watched last night, *Ironjawed Angels*. That movie blew me away. It was about the women's suffrage movement. Hillary Swank played the main character and she was incredible. It showed me how we had to fight for rights that should have been ours to begin with. Who took these rights away from us? Who started that? The right to vote suffrage movement started in 1912 and ended in 1920 when a woman's right to vote finally passed. I recognized that fear was at the core of this issue because it was in every dysfunctional system. Fear caused people to kill one another.

The answer has and will always be love. Love is where God is. It is our belief in separation that has caused us this anguish. It is our belief that we can be annihilated and that we no longer exist when the body is gone. We go to war and kill innocent people. Fear also exists in Western Medicine and I saw that in my 30 years of nursing.

3-24-2012

An empowering lesson I learned from hospice and watching people die was to live my life to the fullest each day. That played a huge part regarding our decision to go on this wonderful family cruise. We just pulled into port from our amazing six-day Caribbean cruise. It was an incredible time with our kids. I had my plant medicine with me in edible form, so I was able to let go and enjoy myself. It was the greatest gift and I was grateful that I listened to my inner wisdom that told me to bring it in spite of my husband's advice that I should leave it home.

I have found that when I do my Sadhana in the morning – my mantra meditation to achieve my purpose in life – everything flowed much better for me. My energy was magnified when I did it over the water on this cruise. The sun was rising over the horizon as I meditated on the deck. I was reflecting about how my scarcity consciousness came to the surface when we were making the decision to take all five kids and their spouses on this cruise. I was so glad that I pushed through that fear of spending money. I let go of the money and magic started to happen. It was such a joy to watch our kids having a great time together singing karaoke. I have two sons from my prior marriage and Gary has two sons and a daughter from his prior marriage. They were able to get to know one another better on this cruise. It was worth every penny we spent on it.

I knew that God had a plan for my life and that I simply needed to surrender to it. My attendance in a 12-step program helped me put the focus on myself. My meetings also helped me have a relationship with my higher power and continual attendance would always be my spiritual lifetime journey.

CHAPTER 49

Self Love

~ ❋ ~

5-23-2012

I was so aware of my growth during these past two years since I retired. My Aunt Toni came to visit me again in spirit. She was so happy and told me she was here to help me.

I frequently enjoyed sitting at my favorite beach, Crystal Cove, located six miles north of Laguna Beach. I marveled at the divinity all around me. I loved the magnificence of the ocean; the warmth of the sun on my shoulders; the waves crashing over the rocks; and the sound of little children laughing and playing. I sat in this place of self-love because I had given myself the gift of retirement at 64-years-old.

I began to really love myself and part of that loving kindness was allowing myself to buy an iPhone. When it was time to replace my cell phone, I consulted my pendulum. It said, "Yes" to the iPhone even when I could have chosen a free phone. I was accustomed to not spending money on myself, but I went with the iPhone anyway. Having access to the voice memo-recording feature on this cell phone was instrumental in the development of this book. That was how I was able to tell my story – the story of watching people die and watching the pain of family members scrambling to do everything they could.

All in all, God is writing this book - I simply needed to just get out of the way.

6-24-2012

A few days ago, my cell phone rang and I recognized the number to be my patient Carolyn's daughter. It was an inconvenient time to talk and I did not answer because my hands were wet from washing dishes. She did not leave a message and I did not call her back. There was a part of me that wanted to put hospice behind me. It was difficult to witness a bedbound woman, who was two years older than myself, and to watch the codependence in her daughter which was the part of me that I did not like. I made great strides in putting myself first since my 12-step program taught me self-love.

I have read that a master teacher of Kundalini yoga said she was raised in a home where her parents grew cannabis and she was an avid fan of smoking it daily. She said that the need for it fell away as she progressed in her Kundalini yoga practice. Maybe that will happen for me as I evolve in my yoga practice. Nevertheless, I could love myself for this path that I had chosen in this lifetime.

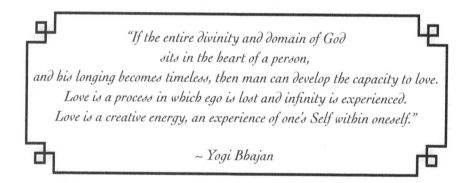

"If the entire divinity and domain of God
sits in the heart of a person,
and his longing becomes timeless, then man can develop the capacity to love.
Love is a process in which ego is lost and infinity is experienced.
Love is a creative energy, an experience of one's Self within oneself."

~ Yogi Bhajan

CHAPTER 50

Mom's Decline

8-28-2012

Last year, I decided to have an important discussion with both of my parents regarding their wishes for end-of-life care. Working in hospice made me realize how important it was to have these talks with our parents. Both of my parents had advanced directives, but I felt these forms were not specific enough for end-of-life issues. I inquired if they would want to be on a ventilator if they were not able to breathe on their own. They both definitely said, "No." I also asked if they would want a feeding tube inserted in their stomachs if they had a severe stroke with a poor prognosis. Again, they both responded, "No." With that, they both wrote their wishes on the advanced directive so they would be honored if those situations arose.

I was appreciative that I knew what my parents' wishes were because my mother had continued to decline. They put Mom on antibiotics again for a urinary tract infection and then she fell down in the bathroom. Inevitably, it was time to look at caregiver options.

In other cultures, like American Indians, when it was the elder's time to make their transition, they went "out to pasture." Hospice was originally set up that way with no aggressive treatments. Was the use of antibiotics considered an aggressive treatment? I thought so. I would rather see my mother take a holistic cranberry supplement, like a CranActin tablet, instead of all those antibiotics. It was so difficult watching both of my parents decline. We were very fortunate that my dad took care of my mom so far.

9-21-2012

How amazing it was to be a part of this dawning of the Age of Aquarius, September 1, 2012. I began my Kundalini yoga teacher training on September 14th. How powerful and profound this time was and it just felt super amazing! I believed this path would help me deal with my mother's decline as well as other challenges the future held for me.

10-12-2012

My visit to Chicago was extremely intense. I arrived four days ago and Mom was slipping fast. I saw it and wanted to run away from it all, but I knew I was an important part of this family. I was so glad I had my hospice experience because it was helping me through this. I saw the signs of stress on my dad's face from the long hours of caring for Mom. This week Mom had another bout with diarrhea and Dad had to get up three times a night for two nights in a row to change her diaper. He was drained.

Both of my sisters were trying to come up with a caregiver solution since mom was quickly declining and it was having a toll on my dad. We visited an assisted living place that my youngest sister, Angela, had found. It looked great, but Mom did not qualify due to her high needs.

I told Angela the story about arranging a five-day respite for Mom with the hospice social worker Richard so it would give Dad a break. Mom sounded skeptical about it, so I decided to arrange it during my stay so I could check out the place. When I called Mom back to see if she would like the respite care, she exclaimed, "I don't want to go to a nursing home, not even for two days." I dropped it and called Richard back and told him to cancel the room.

Mom always sought out attention, so I thought she would ultimately like a nursing home, but she was full of fear and I needed to honor her wishes. I needed to Let Go of being the codependent daughter as I was attached to the outcome. I wanted to fix everything for everybody and realized I was not God.

This health care system was a plan that made people think that they were sick and would be fixed with their poisonous drugs. My mom's bowels were so messed up because she took all those drugs over the past 40 years. In my opinion, it destroyed her body – especially the cardiac medication.

Last year at this time, my mom's Lincoln Financial Universal policy became due. What a rip-off that was! Mom was against this policy, but Dad urged her to switch from her whole life policy to this one. She surrendered the policy that she paid into for 20 years. She gave Lincoln Financial the $19,000 cash value which paid the premium for all those years. Then when that cash was used up, her policy became due to the amount of $458 a month! I figured that Mom was going to transition soon and told her I would pay her monthly premium and her caregiver costs as long as she would name me as the primary beneficiary on her Lincoln Financial policy.

When I projected into the next couple of years what the costs were going to be, it was well beyond my comfort zone. Her expenses would be $1,500 for caregiver costs plus another $500 a month – that was just for part-time day help. I was beginning to see the need for night care as well. I shared with my mom that I could no longer pay these bills and that I also wanted her to put the Lincoln Financial policy back the way it originally was with Dad as the primary beneficiary. When the time came, the rest could be split up among us kids. I called Lincoln Financial and asked them to send a new beneficiary form to Mom.

I was dealing with guilt because I became the codependent who ran to the rescue. Sometimes, I thought that my parents raised me this way in order to manipulate me. My dad asked if I would sit with mom next Monday and I told him, "No, I can't." He had a surprised look on his face. Then I said, "I'll let you know later. Let's see how things go." He wanted to save money on a caregiver. I told him that I had a bad back from my herniated disks and that the doctor did not want me to lift patients.

Later, I received a call from Dad asking if I would sit with Mom on Friday from 11:00 a.m. to 3:00 p.m. I replied, "I'll think about it and let you know later." Thank God I did. I found out that her caregiver, Jill, was scheduled to work that Friday. Jill picked me up and we visited with Mom. I decided to have Jill drop me off two blocks away from the house and walked for 15 minutes until my dad left, so I would not have to face him. He was so manipulative and so was my mom. I was looking at myself during this trip and realizing just how much my parents tried to control me. They were not comfortable with the new Mary, who looked after her own needs, honored her health and spared her back from further injury.

I enjoyed spending time with my grandson, Mikey, and my daughter-in-law, Holly. I slept in until 10:00 a.m. after doing my daily spiritual practice of Sadhana. I talked for an hour with Angela and we had a very rich and deep conversation about our parents and our mother's declining health.

Holly, Mikey and I decided to go to the Little Red Schoolhouse, a museum and wildlife refuge. I called Mom and told her what our morning entailed and I added that we had plans to go play with little Mikey. She said, "Your father has been waiting for you." Immediately, I felt the guilt. My father had an agenda – to ask me to sit with Mom on Friday.

10-14-2012

Yesterday, we celebrated Mom's birthday early. We ordered Portillo's beef and sausage and my son, Mike, brought an ice cream cake from Baskin Robbins. The cake was yummy! It was wonderful to be with my family and celebrate another year with my dear mother. I had some anxiety, so I did a yogic breathing exercise called Breath of Fire in the bathroom for three minutes until my arms hurt. It made a tremendous difference in my vibration and mood and I was glad I took care of myself.

It was becoming harder to watch my mom's demise. Her dentures did not fit because she lost so much weight, so we all chipped in to get her dentures relined. It made me happy to share with the expense. Upon witnessing my mother's poor health, I made a firm resolve to keep my body healthy. I have always believed that we are as young as our spine, so I intend to keep mine flexible and young with Kundalini yoga.

It was wonderful to have the babies with us. Dominick just turned one and Mikey was so cute running around. They played well together and both wanted the same truck. Mikey relented and went to another car. It was so cute to watch.

Mike and I had massage appointments in the morning and I wanted to treat him to breakfast. I needed to spend time with Angela and I decided to take Dad's car to her house. Maybe Jill could take my dad to the senior center and I could arrive there later. I also wanted to have time to see my friend, Peggy, before I left back home to California. I was going with the flow and surrendering to God's will because it was so much easier that way. I did not have to control anything and that brought me serenity.

CHAPTER 51

Home Again

———— ❋ ————

10-16-2012

Tomorrow, I would be going back home and I was anxious to see
Gary and my two cats. I was looking forward to the next Kundalini
yoga teacher training. I was so proud of myself that I did my daily
Sadhana because it was making a huge difference in my life. I was
more centered and balanced. Angela said she noticed the changes in me.

11-26-2012

So many wonderful things are in my life such as my granddaughter,
Kayla. She is the firstborn child of my oldest son, Tom, and his lovely
wife, Tuey, who lived in San Diego.

November 18th was a magical day. I received a call from Tom at
6:30 a.m. while we were doing Sadhana. He said they were at the
hospital and Tuey's labor started at 4:00 a.m. It was unclear whether
I could be in the delivery room. Gary said to not rush off and miss
my Kundalini yoga teacher training class. My intuition said to call
my friend Betsy, who assisted women with childbirth for many years.
She helped me reason things out and I made the decision to leave at
8:30 a.m. I drove to Seventh Chakra Yoga to drop off Gary's stuff that
was in my car. I recognized my reluctance to do so and was glad I did.

I drove down to San Diego and arrived at 10:30 a.m. I went out for breakfast with Tom and then we went to Tuey's room. I kissed her forehead and greeted her mom and then we went to the waiting room so Tuey could nap. Shortly afterward, we received a text message that she was dilated at 9.5 centimeters and we went up to see her. She had received the epidural at 4 centimeters and was somewhat comfortable as she started the pushing process. I was able to see the crowning of the baby's head as Tuey pushed while sending Reiki energy to her. We watched in the mirror. Tom was at her left leg and encouraging her. He was wonderful! The doctor came at the appropriate time. Tuey pushed for an hour and I watched Kayla come into this world. It was magical and miraculous and I cried tears of joy! She was perfect and I was so happy for all of us.

When I was doing Reiki during the delivery, the doctor said, "Send some my way!" Someone else said, "It is filling the room." The doctor was familiar with Reiki and that impressed me. Tom was able to cut the umbilical cord and held his daughter. They put Kayla on Tuey's stomach. Then, it was my turn to hold her. What a joy that was! I was so grateful that I came when I did because Tuey delivered at 2:42 p.m.

It was time to have dinner and my plan was to drive Tuey's mom and myself to a Thai restaurant. I could not find it and I got out of the car and asked for directions from a woman who was standing on the sidewalk. We found the place and had a great meal. I brought back a dinner for Tom and the nurse and that felt good to treat them.

I had difficulty sleeping this evening. I woke up at 12:30 a.m. and took five drops of plant medicine at 1:30 a.m., but still could not sleep. I did Sadhana from 3:00 a.m. to 6:30 a.m. I talked to Tom at 8:30 a.m. and told him I needed to sleep. I wanted them to have some time alone. Tuey's mom and I got there later in the afternoon and stayed for six hours.

The next day was when they were coming home. Tuey's mom stayed at the condo and I went to the hospital and brought some food for us. Tuey had multiple visits from the nursing staff and we finally left the hospital in the late afternoon. Kayla was so cute in her new outfit and they put her in the car seat I had bought for them.

It was difficult to leave my new granddaughter to return home, but I decided it was best because I preferred driving when it was light outside. I took care of myself. I chose to drive the scenic route of Pacific Coast Highway and stopped in Dana Point. I continued my adventure to Crystal Cove in order to marvel at the sunset and gave thanks for my beautiful granddaughter and for three magical days with all of them.

12-3-2012

I could not sleep. It was 1:30 a.m. and my right hip was hurting me. Gary and I went to the movies last night to see *Life of Pi* with Priya and a group from our Kundalini yoga studio. It was fabulous! We went to Corner Bakery to talk about the movie. When I mentioned my hip, Jennifer said it was related to money; adding that, I should journal about it and ask my hip and back to speak to me about what was going on.

I felt guilty that I changed my mind about Mom's life insurance premium. I paid it for a year and decided I could not handle $2,000 a month. I questioned my pendulum if I should continue to pay her premium and it responded, "No." I had many fears about money and it was something that I continued to work on.

I was angry that I allowed myself to get into this mess in the first place. It was a burden to pay this amount every month for her. I was codependent with Mom. It was always, "Mary to the rescue." I only wanted to protect her from the pain of a decision she had made in 1995, when she took out this policy. I called Angela to work through this issue.

Maybe I needed to talk to my mom about this, but I was not sure how to do it. The proceeds from her policy could be put to use for end-of-life expenses that we could not yet foresee. My mom told me that she could not thank me enough for all that I had done for her while I paid the premium. I thought that I wanted to be free of this burden, but I did not have the nerve to tell her.

I took ten drops of plant medicine tincture that I purchased at the dispensary in California with my medical cannabis license. It helped me to relax and I fell back to sleep. It was close to 2:00 a.m. and the alarm was not set for morning Sadhana. Maybe I would sleep in and do it later. I struggled with guilt and berated myself regarding Sadhana. I loved what my yoga teacher, Priya, said, "Guilt never serves anyone, especially when doing Sadhana."

I was still thinking about that policy. I needed to find a way to stay out of it and to rid myself of this guilt. It was not my responsibility to take care of my mother. She had her savings and it was time for her to tap into it to pay this premium. Apparently, this was her journey. She had her own God and I was not it. How freeing was that? If everything was in divine order, then my mom's policy and my involvement in it would be, too. I was glad that I made the decision to be free of it and that was progress.

I remembered that I felt confused that Mom was not dying like the shaman had predicted. Who knew how long she would live? My brother-in-law, Jim, thought she would pass in January. Roxanne thought it would be sooner than that. Her soul knew and she still had work to do and so did I. The lessons were that I could not save her and I needed to use my energy for my own healing. I would continue with my chiropractic treatments and Heller work. I needed to focus on healing my back problem.

12-15-2012

Yesterday, on my birthday, I felt angry, upset and despondent over the killing of 22 innocent children at Sandy Hook Elementary School in Newton, Connecticut. I could not wrap my head around a person who could do something like this. I think of my children and grandchildren and the pain would be unbearable. I prayed for all involved and for healing of this planet.

Years later I heard George Strait's beautiful song *"I Believe"*. His song was about the Sandy Hook tragedy and the belief in the divine and the strength that came from faith. When I heard that song, I had tears in my eyes and wanted to run away. Instead, I prayed for all those people who lost a loved one. I also prayed for an end to people killing one another.

12-31-2012

This is the last day of 2012. Ten days ago, my mom's hospice revoked her because of our family. My sister had a question about Mom's medications and called hospice. They would not talk to her because they already discontinued her service. My sister was offended and wanted me to get the name of the top person at hospice so she could make a complaint. I agreed because I felt guilty about not being there and my sister was doing so much. But later, I did not feel like getting into the energy of criticism. Instead, I wanted to be in the place of gratitude. I reflected back on the 20 months of service Mom had received and how much my parents had benefited from having someone to call when a crisis arose. I told my sister I changed my mind and I was choosing love and gratitude.

Hospice kept my mother out of the hospital which was a huge advantage. Going to a hospital never helped Mom and made her condition worse with all the antibiotics they gave her. Those antibiotics destroyed the good bacteria in her gut and caused diarrhea. At this stage of her life, did she really need to go through another procedure?

Dr. Ira Byock wrote in his book, *The Best Care Possible,* "In general, our health care system doesn't do a good job of helping people deal with the burden of illness. Striking medical advances have not been matched by proficiency in preserving comfort and quality of life for people who are ill and their families." I felt that my role in hospice was providing that comfort and quality of life for my patients. That was why my job was so rewarding. Hospice was truly a gift for my mom and dad.

I knew that Odyssey Hospice was a blessing to my girlfriend, Sharon. Her mother-in-law was declining and the nursing home was constantly sending her back to the hospital. The family did not want that anymore. The social worker told her to request hospice and she did. She requested Odyssey and had an incredible nurse named Margaret, who happened to be my mother's first nurse in May 2011. I sent Odyssey a thank-you card yesterday for all the wonderful care they gave my mom. I mentioned how my mom would call them angels and how much my 91-year-old dad benefited from hospice being there for him day and night. I wanted her service to end on a positive note and I was glad I sent the card. Yesterday, my sister informed me that they found another hospice and began utilizing the service.

I was wondering what I should do. I have Kundalini teacher training in 12 days and would love to attend. I chose not to panic and would see how everything transpired.

CHAPTER 52

Losing My Mom

1-1-2013

Mom had a visit from her new hospice nurse. The nurse felt that my mom had two weeks to live. I knew that could be very inaccurate. During my career, I remembered when families would ask me to predict how long their loved one had and often I was wrong. I felt it was better to say two weeks because it would wake them out of denial. Family members would then have the opportunity to make their visit to say their good-byes while the patient was still coherent. Often, the patients who I thought had longer to live died quickly and those who I thought were at death's door would rally back. It was up to their individual soul when departure took place.

My Kundalini yoga teacher training is January 12th and 13th and it was important for me to be there. It was not like I had tickets to a play and did not want to miss it. It was about healing myself and seven generations past as well as seven generations forward.

I needed to talk to my group about my mom's condition and my continued struggles with my plant medicine. The Kundalini yoga book said plant medicine constricted the cerebral spinal fluid. When I asked my pendulum, it said it did not do that. I was playing the martyr and was not allowing myself to enjoy my plant medicine because I felt that I was not allowed to due to Kundalini yoga.

The yogis were warned not to teach Kundalini yoga openly. They said it would mean certain death and that was false information. Yogi

Bhajan took it to the West because he had a strong calling and he taught it openly. He did not die because he taught it. It turned out they were wrong – just like they said that the use of cannabis was not in alignment with yoga. I think it was for me and it was my path. It was my medicine and my truth.

I attended my spiritual meeting and the topic was "One Day at a Time." That was exactly what I needed to hear. It had to be one day at a time. I had to trust that God had a plan and I was connected to my mom whether or not I was there physically. She and I had a connection and we would continue to have a connection because there is no death. She would speak to me from the other side because I asked her to do that for me. She said she would and I am getting chills as I write this.

I knew that I was in a place of fear when I would continue to worry about what was happening with my mom. She had this rectal abscess and it needed to be drained. They had her on antibiotics which did not help. They finally took her to the hospital and had it drained, but I could not understand why they would not take her to the clinic. Hospice was authorizing it and I did not know what needed to be done.

I needed to keep working my 12-step program as it really encouraged me to stay on track. It made such a difference in my life by keeping my side of the street clean and that was what it was all about.

1-11-2013

I decided to attend teacher training tomorrow and bought a ticket to fly to Chicago on Tuesday, January 15, for two-and-a-half weeks. I was a bit edgy lately and I knew I felt stressed about this trip and my mother's decline. I felt that Mom was holding on until I arrived. I had a phone conversation with Dad today and he still wanted to believe that Mom was going to make it. He was doing okay for now, but I worried about his health and the stress this caused him.

My sister arranged for a full-time caregiver and that was good. It sounded like the caregiver was up all night with Mom. Mom would soon be free of her body that was worn out. I felt that I would have a greater connection with her when she crossed over to the other side.

I chose to stay with Mike, Holly and my adorable grandson, Mikey. I would be able to see Mikey every day and that brought a positive light on the situation.

1-14-2013

Mom died yesterday at 8:00 p.m., Chicago time. I finished my Kundalini yoga class on Sunday at 5 p.m. I did not look at my cell phone during the day because I knew it might be filled with bad news. I checked my voice message when I was in my car and Angela's message asked me to call her. I immediately called her back and she told me our dear mother passed. I burst out crying. The pain in my heart was unbearable and my sweet husband held me in his arms while I sobbed. At that moment, I had a deeper understanding of the quote from *The Prophet* by Kahlil Gibran, "Ever has it been that love knows not its own depth until the hour of separation." That time of separation from my mother was filled with bleak despair.

I struggled with the fact that I was not there when Mom transitioned, however, I sensed that she wanted me to be at the Kundalini yoga teacher training. I really wanted to be there for her since my sister thought she had two weeks to live; therefore, I thought I had time. I figured I could do the teacher training and fly out on Tuesday, but God had a different plan.

As a matter of fact, there was nobody in the room with Mom when she left this world. I knew that patients often did that. They would transition when everyone was gone because the energy of their loved ones kept them on the earth plane. When they were alone in their room, they were with God and the angels. That was how my Mom wanted it and I had to accept that. Meanwhile, I was filled with the sweet memories of her love and devotion.

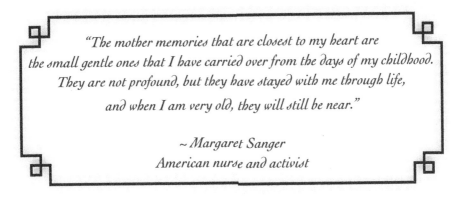

*"The mother memories that are closest to my heart are
the small gentle ones that I have carried over from the days of my childhood.
They are not profound, but they have stayed with me through life,
and when I am very old, they will still be near."*

*~ Margaret Sanger
American nurse and activist*

I felt Mom around me and I received wonderful messages from her about how she loved me. I felt her love and the message that she wanted me to have this time with my yoga teacher training. She was always so caring, loving and kind. Those attributes became more evident to me as I matured. She had so many demons from her childhood that she never talked about. I tried to get her to talk about her life, but she just would not share it with me. One day, I asked her what her most pleasant memory of her childhood was. She said it was when they had company visit. My mother loved people just as much as I did.

My sister, Roxanne, lived 40 minutes away and went home early the night my mom passed. Angela, who lived an hour-and-a-half away, was there with mom. She and my dad were not in the room when my mom made her transition. My youngest brother, who lived in Wisconsin, could not arrive until Tuesday morning because of his work schedule. As for my brother Sam, we never knew what to expect from him. It seemed like every family had one member that drove others nuts.

I chose to do my Sadhana and finished packing this morning. Both of my sisters had really stepped up to the plate and I would help in whatever way I could. They were awesome through this whole thing. It was beautiful to watch this wonderful relationship they had with my dad because so much had been healed. I was very thankful for that and for all of them in my life. Perhaps, I might stay eight days. It was terribly cold in Chicago in January and it most definitely made me appreciate the weather in California.

This was the cycle of life. It was my turn to lose my mother. I had watched it over and over again with people who lost their moms on hospice. I observed all the dynamics and I knew it was going to be my turn someday. Well, here it was. I cried my tears and felt my pain in order to not stuff it down. Tears were a part of life and that was just how grief was.

I flew out of California at 12:15 p.m. and arrived in Chicago at 8:00 p.m. I would deal with whatever needed to be dealt with. I knew I had to put aside this guilt and remorse because it was all in divine right order.

Our family spent the next few days making the final arrangements for Mom's wake and funeral. When I saw my dad, I brought up the subject of Sam. I asked him what he wanted and Dad said he wanted Sam to be notified about our mother's passing. I said, "Yeah, we all agreed to that." I paused. "Do you want to make the call or do you want me to?" Dad confirmed that I would be making the call.

Prior to making the call, I prayed out loud with Stuart and my dad. I sent Sam love and light because that was what the great spiritual teachers were teaching me – to love others. I was able to look at my family through the eyes of love.

First, I organized on paper what I needed to say in case I got his voicemail. I made the call. His phone rang and I eventually received his voicemail. I said, "I am sorry I have sad news to tell you. Our mother left her body on Sunday night at 8:00 p.m. Her last half-hour was very peaceful and nobody was in the room when she passed. I know that she is joyous and free and she no longer has any pain, which was good. I am glad she has no more pain." Then I gave Sam the details about the wake and funeral and closed with, "Hope to see you there." My dad was so appreciative that I made that call and he responded with, "Oh my God, you are so gifted!" I replied that it came from God.

1-17-2013

It was 7:00 a.m. and we were laying our mother to rest at 12noon. Yesterday was the wake and many people attended, including the neighbors that used to live on our block. I saw faces that I recognized but could not remember their names. It was good to see everybody and people reconnected with each other. It was the most amazing service, but it was a long day. It started at 3:30 p.m. and ended at 9:00 p.m.

My ex-husband and his new wife showed up at Mom's wake and he seemed to be doing well. I was happy for him. I came across a couple of pictures and put them aside to give to him and he was appreciative of that. One of the pictures was of him and his parents. The other picture was of him with our two sons. He was a good Daddy and we simply did not give our marriage enough attention. That was why I insisted on having a Thursday date with my current husband and it has been such a wonderful gift. We take a day off and go play. That was what couples needed to do together.

It was hard to see Mom lying in that casket when I first walked in. I burst into tears. We all did. It looked like her, but then again it didn't. The toughest part was when my dad was up at the casket and he kept saying between his sobs, "You look so adorable, you look so adorable." It was so difficult to witness my dad's pain and I wanted to do anything I could to ease his burden. My heart broke for him. He was married 68 years to my mom. How often did we hear that?

My friend, Sherry, channeled my mother this morning. I told Sherry that my mother would have been proud of the wake. She said, "Are you kidding, Mary? She's here right now and she was there and was very joyful. She is now running through this field of beautiful purple and blue flowers." Purple is my favorite color and blue was my mom's favorite color. I was at peace and happy that she was free. Amen.

As for myself, I cried at intervals. Something would trigger the tears and I would let them flow. I would cry; then I would be okay; and then it would come again. It was the grieving process that I witnessed as a hospice nurse.

I was leaving this Wednesday and that gave me some time to do things. I was breaking through fears left and right. I found that there was nothing on the other side except for love and light whenever I broke through my fears.

1-18-2013

Sam did not show up for Mom's wake or funeral. My dad expressed his anger and felt hurt. My heart broke for my dad, but I was relieved that we were spared family conflict and drama. I wondered what today would bring. One thing was for sure – it made me so much closer to my dad and siblings.

A funny thing happened when we went to the cemetery. My brother, Stuart, kept too much of a distance between his car and the one in front of him. He turned into the wrong driveway and went to the wrong section of the cemetery. Of course, the 20 cars that followed behind him had to follow him back! We had a good laugh about it.

I made the decision to stay overnight with my dad at our family home because we did not want him to be alone. It was very painful to look into Mom's bedroom with a vacant bed where she used to sleep. I could not bring myself to even step inside her room. I could only imagine how tough it would be for my dad's new life as a widower. We talked about getting a homemaker for two hours a day to make a meal for him and do light housekeeping. Most likely, Dad would not want that and we would honor his wishes.

It was such a hard thing to lose my mother and it was really unbelievable to see her in a casket. When I looked at her body, it was only a shell anyways. Even though she was so sick, those last few weeks were really difficult right after Christmas. Actually, it started on Christmas day when she could not go to my sister's house because of her bowel problems. She was in a lot of pain and had three fistulas that were full of pus. They drained two of them and could not get to the other. I never understood why people had to go through pain. I knew there was a divine plan and I also knew that God was love.

I am taking good care of myself. I continued doing my morning Sadhanas and it made a huge difference. I did my stretching and my back exercises. I recognized I needed to continue this to keep my back strong.

1-21-2013

I will be flying home in two days. Initially, I was flying home on Friday, January 25th and I was very proud of myself for making that change in my airline flight.

It became easier to keep my center on this trip because after doing my Kundalini yoga every morning, I would smoke cannabis in the afternoon to deal with all the family dynamics and the anxiety that went along with it. All I needed to do was to let go. It was all in the breath; the breath was about letting go.

I was channeling my brother Sam and I was concerned about him. I decided to send him pictures and the memorial card of my mother's so-called passing; but, really, she just left her body.

When I indulged in my plant medicine, I could really channel my mother. When she visited me, she appeared as this young woman. She told me that the Kriya that I was doing for the pituitary was really powerful and it was opening up my master gland that was working on all the glands in my body. This Kriya was very special and felt good on my back, too. My mom also said that she would be with me and assist me in writing this book. Ironically, Sherry channeled that same message from my mother.

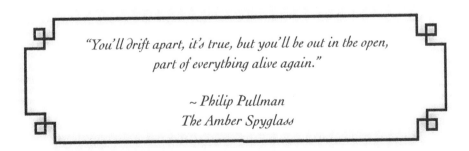

"You'll drift apart, it's true, but you'll be out in the open, part of everything alive again."

~ Philip Pullman
The Amber Spyglass

Here we go with the story of my family. There was abuse, but I came to realize that we were all victims of victims. My parents were abused, too. Each generation appeared to get better because people saw how their parents raised them. They decided that they would do something better. I would like to think it was the evolution of mankind. It was all divine.

I treated everybody to dinner yesterday at Buca di Beppo and we had a great time. It was interesting how it all played out. We reminisced about our beloved mother, especially the love and devotion she showed to all of us. I was feeling deep sadness about losing her and wished she could have been healthy and happy at the end of her life.

During dinner, I asked my dad if he saw any changes in me and he said, "Yeah, absolutely. You are not in touch with reality." I laughed and thought it was the funniest thing I had ever heard. My dad did not understand spirituality and that was okay. I loved and accepted him while no longer seeking his approval. I realized that reality was what I made of it; it was where I put my thoughts. It was all about letting go and connecting to our divine source.

My mother also agreed in my decision when I chose not to take Medicare Part B because it was about going to the doctor. I knew my blood pressure would be elevated when I was stressed and I had no desire to jump on the medication wheel. I remembered when I was waiting in my chiropractor's office and leafing through a book about pharmaceuticals. It stated that many years ago, the parameters for hypertension was 200/100. Needless to say, the big pharmaceutical companies wanted to sell more medications and they lowered the parameters to 140/90. I did not know how true that was, however, I found it quite interesting. I recalled that about 70% of all my patients were on hypertensive medications.

I had a strong message from my mother to deliver the pictures to my brother, Sam. There were many, many photographs that my mother had. I sat down and went through all the pictures. I divided them into five piles for each one of my siblings and placed them in bags. I said to my son Mike, "I received this channeled message from my mom and I would like to go deliver these pictures to Sam. Would you do me a favor and accompany me?" Mike's response was, "Well, you know Mom, you could simply mail it to him." I shared with Mike, "I could do that, but I feel like Grandma wanted me to do this so I could check up on him." He said that he would come with me and when my daughter-in-law came into the room and heard this, she said she would go, too.

We packed everything up for my little grandson and took him over to his other grandma's house. Then, we drove over to Sam's apartment.

When we arrived at Sam's apartment, we rang the bell. He did not answer. I called him and left a message on his voicemail. I told him that I had some pictures for him and left them in his mailbox.

The three of us decided to get something to eat. Shortly after the server took our order, my brother called. I told him which restaurant we were at and invited him to have lunch with us. As the food was arriving at our table, my brother showed up. We greeted each other and I was pleasant. We started looking at albums he brought and we reminisced about the past. I asked him about his life and after we were done, we all hugged each other and said our good-byes.

I was glad I made this decision to check up on my brother to see if he was okay. Sam did not explain why he did not show up for the wake and funeral. I had a sense that it was too painful for him. He said that he was with his best friend at a bar Friday night and they saluted my mother over some beers, so at least I knew that he received my voice message.

The next day, I took my dad out for breakfast. We had a great talk about family and love. I told him about the lunch we had with Sam and the closure I felt with him. Dad was pleased that I did that.

I was in deep gratitude for my 12-step program. I was able to speak to my sponsor and she was just perfect. She knew about the story of my family and was always there for me. Every time something big came about, I knew I could reason things out with her. This was all happening for a reason; it was all in divine right order.

Walking the path of love was difficult because of the opposition I ran into. Jesus was crucified for walking the path of love. The same thing happened to Martin Luther King Jr. When someone was showing light and was in the path of love, it was a real threat for those who were not on that same path. If someone was in the path of darkness, then they were really threatened by the light. It was a mirror and what was shown was not where they were at because they did not want to look at themselves.

I was happy to be returning to California and back to my wonderful husband. I anticipated feeling his arms around me and comfort me through this. I would be able to pet my cats again. I was also looking forward to soaking up the 70-degree weather instead of the chilly 10-degrees that was my experience in Chicago. I would be leaving before the snow hit on Thursday.

It was all about taking care of myself and putting my needs first. Whatever anybody thought was none of my business. I would continue walking the path of love because that was where God was. I chose not to judge others for their path and would simply continue loving and praying for them because that worked for me. People had their own God and I was not God. It was always interesting when I visited Chicago and I felt good that I found out my brother was okay. It would always be about love and reaching those higher vibrations of love.

1-23-2013

I spoke with a friend about the difficulties I faced during my recent family trip to Chicago. She said something very profound. "You know the so-called mistakes in your life? When I give those over to God and let God handle it from there, that is when the miracles occur. That is when the most growth comes and the most magic comes from those dark moments. When we are in it, we cannot really grasp it. We do not understand because we are in the emotional part of it. But later on, when we look back on it, we see how necessary it was."

Wow! It was about having trust and faith that God had a plan. Just like he had the plan for my mother's transition when I was not the one to be with her. Otherwise, I would have been there. I felt like I had been spared in some ways because she suffered a lot in the last couple of weeks and I did not have to watch her demise.

I began doing a 40-day Sadhana meditation called Akal Mahakal. This meditation enabled a spirit to leave. I was slapping my chest like I was taught because it was a tool to deal with the grief and break the attachment. We were attached with an umbilical cord and that cord would be severed; however, the attachment was still there. We became this innocent victim of an innocent victim of an innocent victim. When I realized that, I realized the truth. There was only room for forgiveness, love and compassion and that was the path that I had chosen to walk.

I have had several challenges with my family, however, I have chosen to show up as love. I sent a text message to my two sisters in which I shared, "I have chosen the path of love, forgiveness and compassion. If that does not meet with your approval, then it will be your issue and not mine. Have a blessed day. I love you." I would continue sending love because that was the answer. I also thought about sending monthly love emails to my family. I would like to send my dad a card once a month telling him how special he was. My motive was to help my family heal and if I showed up as love, then I would be healed and not feel lost because I would not hold on to the resentment and the pain. That was my plan.

2-5-2013

The plane ride home was amazing because I had this message to talk to the flight attendant as I found her rather fascinating to watch. We had this soulful conversation about God and how we put everything above God, whether it was alcohol, sex, shopping or whatever else would distract us from contact with him. I knew I needed to step forward with this book and get it going. That was what this left leg pain was all about – I was afraid to move forward and now I was ready.

As I have mentioned before, I saw what Western Medicine did to my mother's health. I believed she would have had great health if she had not gone the Western Medicine route. Mom had a fallen bladder that could have been resolved by doing Kegel exercises. She had a mesh inserted to solve the problem. Unfortunately, it did not work and she had bowel problems after that. I believed that mesh insertion messed her up as well as all the pharmaceuticals she was on. Could you imagine taking 15 tablets a day? And, she took them faithfully. She was so into that fear mode that she thought something was wrong with her. Yeah, she had high blood pressure, but she was anxious. Maybe if she had smoked some cannabis she would have been fine.

I watched this incredible video called *DMT*. It was about the natural substance that turned on our God-self. It was the most eye-opening documentary I had ever seen and it addressed the whole thing about why something that grew as a plant was illegal. How could they make that illegal? It was because all the people in power did not want us to experience the God-self. They could not control us and the big powers wanted to control us. That was the reason why they made drugs illegal. My mother channeled me that this was true. I gave it over to God and knew that God had the answer for my life.

CHAPTER 53

Aftermath

~ ❀ ~

2-19-2013

Sherry came over a few days ago because I needed some Reiki and she gladly obliged. When she was done, we talked about my mom. She said my mom channeled her that there was a reason for all that was happening with my family. It was so interesting.

I was channeling and receiving messages from my mom with my plant medicine. I was able to see her more clearly and it was the coolest thing. I was eating some blackberries and thinking about how she could not eat anything that had seeds in it because she had diverticulitis. I thought to myself, "I wonder if Mom could eat anything she wants now?" She gently answered me with, "Mary, we do not have stomachs. Where I am, the pleasures are beyond anything you could ever imagine." As pleasurable as food, sex and some other wonderful things on earth were, my mom was having a grand old time. Sat Nam.

I sent my sisters a lovely Valentine's email with my parents' picture on it and thanked them for all they had done. I would like to send a loving email every month with Kayla and Mikey's picture on it as well as a quote from Yogananda. I would do it for 12 months and I believed that it would help my dad as he was going through some difficult times missing my mom.

I had a big index card with everybody's anniversaries and birthdays written on it. I started to cry when I saw my mom and dad's anniversary, September 9. My tears quickly subsided when I felt my mom's presence. My mother comforted me by sharing that it was all about being in the moment. If we go back to the moment of her death, then we were in the past and that brought tears. There was no death. The reality was that being in the moment was all there was.

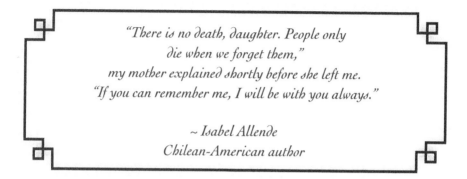

"There is no death, daughter. People only die when we forget them," my mother explained shortly before she left me. *"If you can remember me, I will be with you always."*

~ Isabel Allende
Chilean-American author

5-4-2013

May was my favorite month because it was a month of renewal. The weather was so wonderful except when it was windy like today.

I have been in Kundalini yoga teacher training since September and I experienced an abundance of growth due to Shakti Pad. Shakti Pad was when there was a struggle with the ego and then a plateau would occur. It was about releasing and surrendering to God.

It became vital to have consistency with my daily spiritual practice of Sadhana. What worked best for me was getting out of bed around 4:00 a.m. and driving the four miles to the yoga studio to do Sadhana with my fellow students. I took a big step and volunteered to lead Sadhana. The day before I was to lead, I had so much fear about doing it that I wished I would have been in a car accident and died. Thank God my wish did not come true as it pulled me out of my comfort zone.

Leading Sadhana became a great gift for me and my fellow yogis. It entailed opening the studio doors at 4 a.m.; turning on the lights and music; lighting the candles; creating that spiritual space; and being on the teacher's bench for two hours. We created a space for love because the world needed love.

I was reflecting on relationships lately and found that I was being judgmental again. There really was no room for that in my life as I was just here to show up as love in whatever form that took. I realized that family and friends were our mirrors; if it were not for them, we would not see ourselves as we truly were.

My mother kept coming to me with messages of love and it was pretty cool. I had this really sweet picture of my mom on my altar that was taken five years ago when she was looking pretty good. It was so hard to believe that I had watched her decline as she did.

My mother loved hospice and it was really special those two months that I spent with her in Chicago. I remembered when I gave my mom a foot massage and I looked at the clock – it was 11:11 a.m. I shared with her how special that number was and she said she saw that number frequently. The number 11 represented an angel number. It was a master number and the most intuitive of all numbers. It was also instinctual, charismatic, dynamic and was associated with faith and psychics.

I was so grateful for my beautiful grandchildren. I believed they came from the stars above and were star children. These little people were here to usher in a new world built on love, peace and joy and I believed it was very possible.

6-25-2014

I was shocked that I last journaled 13 months ago and could not believe that I avoided my book for so long. I felt lazy since I retired and I just did not want to work. I saw this book as work until today when I decided to have some cannabis which put me in a creative mood.

I was alone this morning because Gary was at the Kundalini yoga summer solstice in New Mexico until June 29th. I was enjoying our beautiful backyard, which had native plants and fruit trees, as I savored the solitude.

I loved teaching a yoga class called Gentle Kundalini Yoga for the

Back every Wednesday at 3:30 p.m. After a 9-month course, Gary and I became teachers in May 2013. I really appreciated that course as it deepened my experience of Kundalini yoga. Everything continued to improve my spirituality and I found myself in deep gratitude for all the blessings in my life.

7-5-2014

I had an amazing day today. It started with my 12-step meeting in Newport Beach. The group consisted of only women and was very powerful. Initially, I was not going to attend because I wanted to meet a new friend for breakfast. But, I felt that I needed to go to that meeting and I called my friend to change our time to a lunch date in Sunset Beach.

I met my friend, who was an RN, as she wanted to be a hospice nurse. We sat for a couple of hours talking about everything in our lives and I shared about my hospice days before my retirement. So many memories came flooding back. There were so many patients and their families that I shared special memories with.

I reminisced about the time I was able to witness my dear patient, Ngoc, take her last breath. Her body was illuminated and I felt the angels all around us. She chose to leave when all of her family was out of the room and only she and I were left. It was so peaceful and beautiful. The energy of a patient's loved ones kept them on the earth plane because the patient did not want to leave their family. That was why it was so important to reassure their loved ones that they had plans for their future and would be greeted with blissful love. One of my favorite sayings is, "We are not our bodies."

7-16-2014

I needed to breathe and go with the flow of life. My son, Tom, decided to move to Dallas, Texas, in order to provide a better life for his family. Homes are very affordable there; however, I was heartbroken. I was the same age as my son is today when I moved away from my family. What a coincidence.

My beautiful little granddaughter, Kayla, who was 20-months old, was very special to me. She was very cute and learning two languages at the same time – English and Thai. Now, I would be visiting by plane, three times a year, to see her. Luckily, retirement was good to me thanks to my healthy retirement plan. It allowed me to fly to see my grandkids. My life was so full and it would do me good to put it on hold for six days to visit with my family.

Kundalini yoga enlightened me to be more present when I remembered the breath. My favorite was long, slow and deep. I imagined that there was a balloon in my belly. I would start by filling up my belly; next was my chest; and then my shoulders. To exhale, I would go backwards – shoulders, chest and belly. This breathing changed my life and enabled my endorphins to increase because it was the yoga of awareness. I strengthened my nervous and immune systems and it made a huge difference when I kept my core strong. I even felt that I was looking younger, too!

It was such a gift to find a healing yoga set called Basic Spinal Energy Series that healed my back during my morning Sadhana. This was the same yoga set that I taught my students every Wednesday afternoon at the studio in which I trained. My life was much better when I shared with others.

8-1-2014

I received a call from a friend and she told me that her dad was approaching death. He was on hospice, thank God, and they were letting nature take its course. She asked if I would do shamanic energy work on him because she knew of my background and hoped that I could make his transition smooth. I told her I would be honored to serve in that capacity. I arrived at their home and was able to perform shamanic death rites on her dad. He was very peaceful when I left and made his transition three hours later. An abundance of gratitude flowed through my heart that I was of service to others because of the path that I chose … what a gift!

I recalled doing shamanic death rites on Margie's dad before he died. I felt his spirit leave. He died peacefully. I also thought of the time I was doing Reiki on another patient while she was dying and I felt her spirit leave her body, too. Her daughter also saw her soul leave, but the patient was still breathing and that confused me. I left their home for a work-related meeting and, about ten minutes later, I received a call from our office that the patient had died. I could not go back to the patient's home because they needed me at this meeting. These meetings were mandatory from the Federal government to keep our license. I regretted that I did not remain at their home.

8-29-2014

It was two weeks since Tom and his family moved to Dallas. It still broke my heart to think of them living so far away. I enjoyed my drives to San Diego to visit them which I had been doing every month since Kayla was born. When I knew of their plan to move to Dallas, I increased my visits.

Kayla was so special to me because we had a connection on a soul level. When my husband and I took all the kids on a Caribbean cruise in March 2012, I was doing yoga and meditation on the ship's deck before sunrise. I channeled Kayla before she was born. She said, "I'm a little girl and am coming to join your family. I will be the daughter of Tom and Tuey." I told my son and daughter-in-law about the message. They were not yet aware that Tuey was pregnant with Kayla at that moment. Tuey was more of a believer of paranormal phenomena and Tom seemed amused, but open-minded. When it was time for the ultrasound, I told them the baby was a girl.

I had a flight to Dallas already booked for Tom's and Kayla's birthdays. His is November 17th and hers is November 18th. I was going to be there for a week and was looking forward to that.

Prior to my Dallas visit, I would be traveling to Chicago on October 9th to see my first grandson, Mikey. He was such a sweetheart just like his daddy. It was such a joy to watch both of my sons become awesome fathers.

My children have it so much better than my mother's generation. She was filled with fear which was passed on to me. Since I was the oldest, I absorbed it all. It has been my biggest challenge in life to face those fears about scarcity consciousness.

I made the decision to start tithing 10% of my Social Security and IRA disbursements to various charities. My 12-step program was one of the organizations my money went to. It not only saved my marriage, but it saved my life. I attend three to four meetings a week and made some awesome friends.

Sunday is my favorite meeting because we meet on the beach in the morning and I admire the people who attend. Today, six of us stayed after the meeting and went swimming in the ocean. This was a big deal for me because it was about four years ago since I swam in ocean waters. I developed a fear about the waves, but my two good friends took hold of my hands as we ventured into the sea. They were right beside me and encouraged me as we dove through the waves. They helped me face my fear and it was terrific. I felt incredibly empowered and proud that I took a dip into my fear!

My two cats have been such a joy in my life. Sammy is all black and Bobby is a gray tabby. They were rescue cats from the same litter and are 7-years-old. Sammy was the spiritual one and would come into my healing room when I saw clients for shamanic Reiki treatments.

I always knew that animals had healing energy. I felt calmness when they were near and when I would pet them. I knew that someday they would leave their physical bodies just like we did. When that time comes, I would grieve their loss and, eventually, I would get two cats to fill that empty spot. Even though I love dogs, too, I found that cats were easier because I liked their independence. Gary and I appreciated the fact that cats do fine on their own if we decided to get away for a night or two.

9-25-2014

Gary went to Atlanta to visit his daughter, Lindsay, and granddaughter, Zoey. I considered going, but I was not comfortable with Gary's ex-wife being around for the visit. She was living with Lindsay for several months now.

I loved having this time alone and needed it so much. It was like a retreat without leaving home and it gave me time to ponder. I was going to my 49th high school reunion on October 10th when I would be visiting my family in Chicago. What a coincidence that it fell on the weekend I would be there when I booked this flight four months ago. I called Sharon who said she was going to the reunion and arranged for her to pick me up, meet my grandson Mikey, and then head to the reunion.

I would be going to Dallas for Kayla's 2nd birthday in November. I felt a lot of grief when they moved in August. I made a FaceTime call to them every night they were on the road to see where they were on their Dallas journey. They were traveling by car and I was the typical, worrisome mom, but it was reassuring to see their smiling faces on my iPad every night. Kayla was a great traveler and I missed her so much already.

I knew that there were blessings in all of this because Tom was able to keep his job and he would work remotely from home. He would also be flying back quarterly to San Diego for business. I was so excited that I would see him this Sunday because it would give us time alone together.

I knew I had the right man in my life when Gary was supportive about my decision to become a hospice nurse. Others in my life tried to dissuade me from going into hospice because they thought it would be too depressing. I struggled with that concept myself and it was a decision I never regretted.

People tended to look at death as a bad thing, but I refused to since I had seen so much beauty in it. It truly was a graduation to a higher level of being. When my mom was still alive, Sherry channeled a message from my mother's sister who had recently crossed over. The message from my aunt was, "I am light and there is nothing but light." Sherry also channeled that my aunt went to the other side during her spaced-out times with Alzheimer's. She came back to the earth plane when she wanted to connect with her husband and son.

11-24-2014

I came back last Thursday from a 5-day trip to Dallas to see Tom, Tuey and my granddaughter Kayla. It was a wonderful visit and the time spent with them was precious. We went out to eat at many restaurants which we all loved doing. We went to the Perot Museum and it was awesome. I enjoyed giving Kayla a bath every day and cuddled with her at night before bed.

When the time came to return to California, I was excited to be coming home to Gary. I was so blessed to be married to him, but it was not always that way. He has grown in so many ways – actually, we both have. Gary picked me up from the airport and we had lunch at True Food in Newport Beach. When we arrived home, we watched the movie *Practical Magic*. Marriage was what you made of it and when I showed up as love, everything had a way of working out beautifully.

11-27-2014

I had a message from spirit to go to Chicago for Christmas. I started doubting it, but I thought of four good reasons to go …

First, Dad was now legally blind from macular degeneration and lost his independence. I wondered how long he would still be with us. He used to tell me that he would not want to live if he was not able to drive and be independent.

The second reason was Mikey who was three-and-a-half-years-old. He called out for me every night before he went to bed and I was so touched by that. It would be such a pleasure to watch him open his gifts on Christmas Day with his belief in Santa Claus. We would be creating heartfelt moments that would be cherished like sharing Mikey's joy with Mike and Holly from the magic that the holiday would bring. Spending time with Holly was the third reason since she lost her dad last week. Family was what the holidays were all about.

Last, but not least, was that Tom and Tuey were in Dallas and I felt sad that I would not see them this Christmas. Then a thought occurred to me … If other people traveled for the holidays, then I should, too! I would see how I could arrange my schedule.

I needed to step through fear once again. I had not been in Chicago for Christmas in quite a while, not since Tom and Tuey left for Thailand in 2005 which was nine years ago. Tuey had to move back to Thailand because she was on a student visa that was past the expiration date. Tom chose to accompany her back to Thailand and they lived there for three years. Gary and I visited them in Thailand and had a wonderful time. We had the opportunity to spend some romantic time alone in Phuket.

12-19-2014

It is 2:00 a.m. and I could not sleep. Gary and I were in a beautiful hotel in Laguna Beach for our weekly Thursday date.

I typically read in bed, but because Gary shared my bed, I chose not to so I would not disturb his sleep. I did not take a bath because I wanted to be asleep by 9:00 p.m., so I could get up early to watch the sunrise.

I was just irritated today. Parts of our date were magical for me. I enjoyed walking on the beach with Gary while catching the beautiful sunset. We had some great conversation and laughter over a delicious Indian dinner followed by gallery hopping. We returned to the inn and had a patio overlooking the ocean with a gorgeous view. I sat there by myself and reflected on the wonderful memories of my nursing career.

I have chosen to stay in this marriage over and over again. My 12-step program helped me with this. I knew I had to put the focus on myself. It was not always easy to do, but I was much better than I used to be.

Maybe I needed to focus on the good, like my friend Brigid said. This journey was not an easy one, but there was tremendous growth for me living with Gary. That was why he was in my life. No accidents there; it was all divine. Focus on the 70% that was good.

I shut off the alarm that was set for 5:30 a.m. I figured it would be best if I took care of myself and got the sleep I needed. At least I brought this journal, so I could write down my feelings.

12-23-2014

I just could not sleep. Tomorrow was my flight to Chicago to see my family again. I was looking forward to seeing everyone at my dad's house on Christmas Eve when we would all be together. This was the second Christmas since my mom passed away and it was just not the same without her.

I had fantasies about how the five days would be. I simply needed to show up as love and keep my mouth shut. I needed to be in the moment and knew that I could do that easily.

I was glad I had an afternoon flight and looked forward to seeing Mikey tonight! I loved him so much and it was so sweet that he had been calling out for me these past two months. Although I was there in October, I still missed him. It was difficult to have my grandchildren living so far away.

I was able to sleep as long as I needed to because everything was all packed in the suitcase – my gifts, my bio mat, my clothes and some miscellaneous stuff. I was good to go and had good vibes that it would be a fabulous trip!

12-29-2014

I was on the plane flying home again. This really was a wonderful visit. I did a good job by staying in love and acceptance. One of the highlights was surprising my dad on Christmas Eve. Angela videotaped it and it was so precious. It was astounding that my dad was well worth the price of this trip!

It was a joy to be with Angela and her family. She ordered food from Portillo's and it was so delicious! After we ate, we all played the card game Texas Hold 'Em and had a lot of laughs.

We went to Pet Land and I bought Mike a Yorkie-Poo puppy for

Christmas with the crate and all the goodies. They all fell in love with this little guy, especially Mikey who named the puppy Memo. Memo got accustomed to the crate as well as doing his business outside. I was thankful that I had the money to do this for them because it was all about my abundance consciousness.

I loved being able to treat everyone to a nice meal at Rodity's in Greektown on Saturday night. Mike, Holly, Cay, Roxanne, Jim and Dad were my guests. The food was delicious and we had so much fun.

On the way to the restaurant, Roxanne and I sat in the back seat and caught up with each other's lives. She told me about her dreams. We reminisced about Mom and how much we missed her. We talked about the joy we had being with our grandchildren. I gave my sister love and acceptance because we had our own paths to follow.

Christmas day was fun at Holly's mom's house because Cay was so giving and loving. She made a wonderful turkey dinner with all the trimmings. It was great to see Holly's brother, Charles, and her sister, Brenda. I also felt Holly's dad's presence in the home and I was able to channel him. He said he was happy.

Holly really liked the essential oil that Cynthia made for her. She cried when I told her that the blend would help her grieving process. Holly and I hugged and cried together. I loved Holly because she was so good for Mike and brought him valuable lessons.

It was fun to watch Mikey play with his friend Darius. They were so cute together! My connection with Mikey was the best part of this trip and I realized that it did not need to be Christmas because I could do it anytime.

I probably would not travel to Chicago again soon for Christmas, but I was so glad I did this time. It was perfect, except for the stress of gift giving, but even that was not so bad. I decided that I could travel in October, April and June and fly them out to California in August.

1-16-2015

I saw an impressive film, *Words*, and it had a huge impact on me. It portrayed an affluent married couple in a mixed marriage. He was white and she was African American. The film was incredible because the author channeled the book for two years. He poured out his pain on to those pages and I related so well to the story.

Last night we went to see Isha in Northridge. His talk was inspirational and informative. He spoke about following the divine guidance for your life. He also said studies showed that cannabis caused the brain to shrink. I did some research and found opposing views about whether this was true. I asked my pendulum and received a "No." I also asked my pendulum if cannabis caused me any physical harm and I received the same answer.

Today was an eventful day. It began when I woke up startled at 4:30 a.m. because I heard my inner voice telling me to get out of bed to do Sadhana. Gary had already left to the yoga studio to lead Sadhana. I got out of bed and was going to do my own Sadhana, but I was tired. I really wanted to get the extra sleep because I liked going to Dana's 7:00 p.m. yoga class and going out for a bite to eat afterward. I decided to go back to bed and get up later, but unfortunately, I was thinking about the potluck party we were going to host at our home for our yoga friends and all the things that needed to be done in less than two weeks. I quieted my mind and asked God to take over this party. I put earplugs in my ears to block out the outside noise and I surrendered and fell fast asleep. Gary came home around 7:30 a.m. and we cuddled in bed.

I finally woke up at 8:00 a.m. and looked at my cell phone. There was a missed call and voice message from Jessica, a pregnant 20-year-old young lady. I had been volunteering for the past six months as a doula for women who lived in a shelter who needed support. Jessica just left a grunt on the message, so I called her back. She said she was with her baby's daddy when her water broke and they went straight to the hospital. I offered to come to the hospital and she was okay with that. I arrived when Jessica was pushing and her baby boy was born at 10:02 a.m.

Jessica called her mother who came in from Arizona a few days ago to be there for her. I understood that this was a time for Jessica and her mom to bond since Jessica's grandparents raised her. If I had arrived earlier, I would have stepped into the role of mom and wedged

Jessica's mother out of the picture. My belief was that everything was in divine right order.

This experience made me realize that being a doula was not my path, at least for these kinds of situations. It was delightful to be present for the birth, but I felt remorseful that I did not hear my phone ring. Maybe I would do better with women who were being induced because I would know when to show up at the shelter and could plan my life around that. I did not want to leave my warm bed at 2:00 a.m. because it reminded me too much of the on-call work I did for years as a home health and hospice RN.

These were my retirement years and there were many ways I could be of service. I was truly working toward accepting my imperfection and humanness and it was okay how the day unfolded.

3-21-2015

I had a hard time sleeping, so I got up at 4:30 a.m. to do Sadhana. Tonight, was the overnight gong ceremony at the yoga studio, so I really needed my rest this morning.

On Wednesday, I went out for breakfast with Andrea and Dana to work on our flyer for the workshop we were doing. When I pulled into the parking space, I reached down on the passenger side and there was my mom's picture that was missing for a couple of years. I searched endlessly for this picture and could not believe my eyes! About six months after my mom passed, I wanted to make copies to send to my siblings. I guess the time was not right then.

I will be going to Chicago in about three weeks. My mom's picture gave me the message that she was still with me and that I should trust that everything was in divine order. Do I keep showing up as love? The answer was yes.

I loved being with my sons and their families so I made a decision to have a family reunion and fly them all out to California. Tom and I figured out the flights for Dallas and Mike had to decide on times and dates for Chicago. I needed to be patient with them, but I had some anxiety about purchasing airline tickets due to my scarcity consciousness After all, the trip was four months away and I had plenty of time to purchase the tickets at a decent price. I just had to trust in the process that it would work out great.

In 1992, I wrote the following note to myself, imagining what my perspective would be at age 80 ...

Live life as fully as you can. Laugh a lot and have fun. Don't take life so seriously. Be true to yourself. Life is full of risks and you can sit on the shore wondering whether you should set sail forever and never do what you want to do. Life is a challenge. We don't have all the answers; you need to put your faith in God and ask for his guidance in your life. Then, trust that you are exactly where you need to be.

Love the people in your life and let them know how much you appreciate them. Accept their gifts and graciousness. Give freely and willingly. You will never regret that.

Life is full of lessons. Learn by your mistakes and don't expect perfection from yourself or others. We are all learning and growing. You will find that your greatest growth comes from pain. And when God closes one door, he has a better path for you to follow.

Set your children free to be who they are and appreciate their uniqueness. They will return your love in many ways. And above all, love yourself.

3-23-2015

I decided to take myself on a three-day personal retreat. I was not able to get a room at Crystal Cove like I hoped, but I found a cute little place in Laguna Beach at the Crescent Bay Inn. I received great comfort at the ocean with its beautiful climate.

It was so important to have solitude because I still felt Mom's presence in my life and was receiving messages from the afterlife. As I looked back on my life, and especially my days with hospice patients and their families, I was filled with love and gratitude for the life I was given. Life was extremely good!

Epilogue

10-26-2017

Today was my mother's birthday and she would have been 95-years-old. I still miss her so much and would give anything to get a hug and kiss from her. I feel her presence when I become quiet – especially when I am at the ocean. I also receive messages from her, but not as much as I did when she made her transition.

Obviously, many things have taken place in the two-and-a-half years where I ended my book. My dad has been in an assisted living facility for the past two years. His eyesight became very poor due to macular degeneration and it was apparent that he was no longer able to live alone. He has dementia and occasionally asks where my mother is. He is now on hospice for end stage cardiac disease with the same company my mother was with, which is a blessing for everyone.

As I reviewed my life since retirement seven years ago, I am filled with deep gratitude and joy. My views about hospice remain the same because hospice is now keeping my dad out of the hospital and giving him the medical expertise and support in the twilight of his remaining years.

I am still making my trips to Chicago two or three times a year to visit my dad and family. I especially love spending time with little Mikey who is six-years-old. During my last visit, I accompanied him to his first-grade class and met his teacher and fellow classmates. He was filled with pride as he showed me his desk that had colored pens, markers and notebooks as well as the artwork that covered the walls.

As I read through my manuscript, I thought about how much I have grown and changed. I wonder if I would have been a better employee, nurse, wife, friend and mother if I found Kundalini Yoga many years ago. I felt that I would have, however, I started it when I was meant to. I was always striving to live in a higher state of consciousness and understood that it would be an on-going process throughout my life. Showing up as love in my daily life is my goal and continues to be my path.

The family reunion with my two sons and their families was awesome. I was lucky enough to rent a cottage for three days at my favorite beach, Crystal Cove. My grandchildren loved playing and being together. We had great meals at the Beachcomber and enjoyed watching beautiful sunsets over the water. Those memories will live in my heart forever.

I am looking forward to attending Kayla's 5th birthday party in Dallas this November. It seems like yesterday that I watched her entrance into this world. I decided to stay through Thanksgiving, which is a first for me. As my mother used to say quite frequently, it is unbelievable how fast time goes by.

I am working with Balboa Press for the editing and publishing of my book because it is a division of Hay House which I have loved for years. Louise Hay was my heroine and I felt sad about her recent passing. Balboa Press is wonderful to work with and I learned so much through this process. This journey brought up that critical voice telling me that my book was not good enough. I am striving to shut that negative voice and know that I am and always will be on a divine path.

Back in May of 2016, I received an email from Hay House about Robert Holden's Coach Camp that he was presenting in San Diego in June. My inner guidance was shouting at me, "Yes, Yes, Yes – Do this!" So, I listened and obeyed. That Coach Camp changed my life! I told Robert I was going to be one of his groupies and we had a good laugh together. I also attended two more of Robert's Coach Camps and loved each one. During his first workshop, I met some wonderful people who became my good friends.

Shawn Gallaway was the singer at that workshop in San Diego, performing his award-winning song "I Choose Love." His music is transformational and healing. We are good friends and my husband and I hosted him in our home last February for a concert.

I met an awesome woman, Wendy Treynor, who is an author, healer and motivational speaker. Wendy and I also became great friends and did a healing retreat together this past summer.

I had the pleasure of meeting Ian Lynch and John Haggerty at Robert's workshop. Ian, John and Shawn put together an organization called "Rites of Man, Rites of Woman" and are helping to transform this world with their positive message.

When the San Diego Convention Center hosted Louise Hay's 90th birthday celebration on October 8, 2016, I felt a strong calling to be there. Robert Holden was one of the presenters as well as other speakers who I adored. Little did any of us know that this would be the last time we would see Louise Hay who made a short guest appearance. Robert gave a glowing tribute to this beautiful woman who created Hay House and helped thousands of people heal.

Shawn was planning on being in San Diego the day after Louise's birthday celebration. That weekend, he invited me to be part of a support team with Wendy, Ian and John to help put together his workshop "The Dance of the Divine Feminine and the Divine Masculine." Shawn's powerful workshop changed my life and healed old wounds. I was able to rent a house in San Diego for all of us to stay at for four days and we deepened our friendships as we shared great memories and laughter.

I was pleased that cannabis became legal in many states and I am grateful that people have greater access to this natural medicine. As for myself, I still enjoy it occasionally and discontinued my daily use. Kundalini yoga was instrumental in this transformational process and I continue to teach it every Wednesday at our beautiful yoga studio. I am very grateful for this opportunity to help transform people's lives.

I recently returned to teaching Reiki classes in my home. It is a joy to watch my students as they experience this amazing energy for the first time when they practice in my healing room. I also continue to do healing sessions for the people who God sends my way.

I am attending my 12-step meetings on a regular basis. I am on the service board bringing awareness to young people who are in need of the help, love and support through this wonderful organization. I am also a sponsor to many women whom I get to grow with.

In closing, I took a walk at my favorite park where I experienced the miracle of my patient, Dennis, in his butterfly form. I reminisced about that amazing day and how my life has unfolded since then.

I am in deep gratitude that I get to live a life of service to others. Life has been awesome to me as I continue to Let Go and Let God and surrender to the divine flow of the universe.

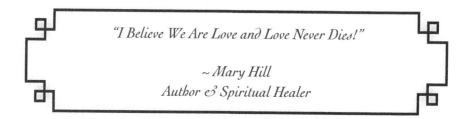

"I Believe We Are Love and Love Never Dies!"

~ Mary Hill
Author & Spiritual Healer

"May His Memory Be Eternal"
George G. Orfanos
96 years young
At Rest January 31, 2018

My awesome dad left his body today. I miss him so much, but feel grateful that I had him for a dad. He was loving, kind and so much fun. There have been some beautiful moments during my time in Chicago along with the tears and grief. I am grateful that I made it to his bedside and got to spend time with him before he passed. He is now dancing in the light and love with my mom who made her transition 5 years ago. I believe we are Love and that Love never dies. 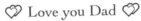 Love you Dad

Mom

Dorothy

Nursing graduation